Joseph F. Berry

Four Wonderful Years

A sketch of the origin, growth, and working plans of the Epworth League

I0023325

Joseph F. Berry

Four Wonderful Years
A sketch of the origin, growth, and working plans of the Epworth League

ISBN/EAN: 9783337097240

Printed in Europe, USA, Canada, Australia, Japan

Cover: Foto ©ninafisch / pixelio.de

More available books at **www.hansebooks.com**

FOUR WONDERFUL YEARS

A Sketch of the Origin, Growth, and Working Plans of the Epworth League

By JOSEPH F. BERRY, D.D.

Editor of "The Epworth Herald"

WITH AN INTRODUCTION

BY THE REV. WILLIAM INGRAHAM HAVEN, M.A.

NEW YORK: HUNT & EATON
CINCINNATI: CRANSTON & CURTS
1893

PREFATORY NOTE.

DURING the past year or two there has been an eager demand for reliable information touching the origin and growth of the Epworth League. Many letters have been received requesting us to supply the important data. The impracticability of writing the information for each applicant suggested the idea of preparing the material in our possession for general distribution.

This little volume does not assume to be a history. It is too early for that. A comprehensive review of the Epworth League movement will be written some day, and the matter which we have gathered in the following pages will be of value to our future historian. We have aimed to tell the story of the organization and development of our League in the simplest possible manner, and to present only such facts as will be of practical use to our young people.

The chapter on "Incidents and Impressions of the Cleveland Conference," written by representatives of the five original societies, will be found particularly interesting.

The first four years of the Epworth League have been very blessed. But we are only starting. More glorious times are just ahead. May every one who reads these chapters resolve to do his very best to help the cause which is doing so much for Christ and his Church !   J. F. B.

CHICAGO, *May* 15, 1893.

CONTENTS.

CHAPTER IX.

CHAPTER X.

CHAPTER XI.

ILLUSTRATIONS.

INTRODUCTION.

"Four Wonderful Years." Who can fail to be interested in this
volume ? It has about it all the fascination that belongs to the story
of origins. One never tires of Genesis, as one never wearies of the
spring. Dull as the heart may be through the stress and storm of
winter, it leaps when it sees the first bluebird, with his "earth tinge"
and "sky tint;" it cannot help it. There is a revelation in the
sight of the presence of Him of whom Jesus says, "My Father work-
eth hitherto." The melody that comes from the throat of the song-
sparrow choir calls for reverence and an attentive ear to a higher
message as truly as the voice from out the bush the Midianite saw
aflame with God. It is the message of the Divine nearness, the
Divine interest. Of course God is with us in the fuller, ampler
labors and experiences of the riper periods of life, but he does not
impress upon the mind his presence as in the first movements when
the earth warms, the trees bud and blossom, the ponds quiver with
their first visitants, and the woods are vocal.

We are as near God in the days of the prophets as in the days of
Abraham, but we feel his touch more vividly in the ever-charming
tales of the first household ; the first hunter ; Methuselah, of many
years ; Abraham, God's friend ; Jacob ; and Joseph, with his lively
vestment. The child, the youth, the man, feels here in these stories
of beginnings the thrill of the supernatural.

So, in our Epworth movement, the days at Cleveland will be ever
memorable to the youth of the Methodism of America and the lands
where the missionaries of the Church in America have gone, because
there God drew near to the consciousness of his servants and said to

them, not "Separate me," but "Unite me the young forces of the Church, that I may use them to hasten the upbuilding of my king-dom." Interesting as these pages will be from the mere human phases of the story, they have their vital interest in the fact that our honored editor and those that assist him here record a fresh manifes-tation of the Spirit's influence, working out the divine plans for the world's salvation. How wonderfully, under the Spirit's guidance, these four years of unification and organization have gone on! What the future is to be He alone knows who holds the keys of the future. It simply behooves us to watch, that, having begun in the Spirit, we may never attempt to be "made perfect by the flesh," but rather mind "the things of the Spirit." Then shall we be the "sons of God." And in this present age, with its imperial problems and possibilities, what is more needed than a well-disciplined host of the sons and daughters of the Lord Almighty?

May this volume help to make the Epworth League such a host!

WILLIAM INGRAHAM HAVEN.

OVERMARSH, *Easter*, 1893.

FOUR WONDERFUL YEARS.

CHAPTER I.

METHODISM AND HER YOUNG PEOPLE.

THE Epworth League is the young people's society of the Methodist Episcopal Church. It is just four years old. *Four wonderful years* they have been. No young people's religious organization has ever enjoyed a more rapid and symmetrical growth. It has caused universal amazement and almost universal congratulation. Think of it! There are now in the Methodist Episcopal Church ten thousand senior and two thousand junior chapters. This includes organizations in all parts of our own country and in Mexico, Brazil, Argentine, Denmark, Norway, Sweden, Italy, Bulgaria, India, China, Japan, and other lands where our Church has planted missions. The membership is already more than six hundred thousand. Besides this, the Epworth League has taken firm root in the Methodist Episcopal Church, South, and in the Methodist Church of Canada. In England, too, the movement has been introduced, and is already received with marked favor. The present rate of growth is rapid. Everywhere the League is winning golden opinions even from those who were at first skeptical about its utility and permanency.

Enthusiasm over the success of the Epworth League has not been confined to the young people. Senior leaders in all departments of our* church life have warmly approved. The bishops, without exception, have said, "God speed the League!" Our college and university authorities, recognizing the movement as a potent agency for stimulating the intellectual activity of the young, have gladly given their indorsement. The editors of our church papers have written columns of encouragement and inspiration. Presiding elders have welcomed the League to their districts and promptly set its machinery in motion. Literal thousands of our most alert and successful pastors have helped the cause forward by their prayers, counsel, and enthusiastic advocacy, and have never been quite so happy as when marching in the vanguard of the Epworth procession. Our senior friends mingle with us at our conventions, participate in our discussions, speak from our platforms, bow at our altars of consecration, unite with us in our songs of gladness, and plan with our leaders for the extension of the work. The cordial expressions of District and Annual Conferences, and the decisive action of the General Conference in giving the League a place beside the other great connectional organizations of the Church, have reflected in a more formal way the friendly sentiment of the entire denomination.

But it must not be supposed that this Epworth League movement is the initial effort of Methodism to promote the social, intellectual, and spiritual culture of her young people. During all the years of her eventful history individual churches have sustained societies for the special benefit of their younger members. In recent years these organizations had multiplied until, in the larger churches, they had become quite common. Many of the distinguishing features of these local societies were retained in the more general organizations, which in turn have been inherited by the Epworth League.

The first movement to provide a uniform organization dates back to the year 1872. Some time previous to that date there had been organized by Rev. Dr. T. B. Neely, in the Fifty-first Street Methodist Episcopal Church, Philadelphia, a Church Lyceum, the chief object of which was to encourage the systematic reading of approved books. Several similar lyceums were formed in neighboring churches, and soon it was thought best, for purposes of mutual cooperation, to unite these in a city union. At a meeting of the board of managers of this central body held March 3, 1872, it was resolved to memorialize the General Conference then soon to assemble at Brooklyn, N. Y., asking formal recognition of the Lyceum. The memorial was presented to the Conference by Rev. W. F. Warren, D.D., President of Boston University, and was referred to a committee. After due consideration the committee made a favorable report, but, owing to the great pressure of business at the close of the session, the recommendations of the committee were not acted upon. At the succeeding General Conference, that of 1876, the request for official recognition was renewed. Owen Osler, M.D., of Philadelphia, was active in calling attention to the need of the Lyceum, and wrote a stirring article on the subject for *The Methodist*, which was widely read and commented upon. The memorial which failed in 1872 was carried to the General Conference of 1876, and was presented to the body by Dr. E. O. Haven, then Chancellor of Syracuse University and afterward bishop. The paper was referred to the Committee on Education, of which Dr. Haven was chairman. Here he earnestly exerted his influence in behalf of the proposed legislation, and, the committee reporting favorably, the Conference adopted *verbatim* the paragraph sent up by Dr. Osler in 1872. The Lyceum was received with much favor in different parts of the Church. It did a good work in stimulating the intellectual life of the young and in promoting a taste for the pure and upbuilding in literature. The organization was destined, however, to give place to the Oxford League, a society which retained the idea of intellectual culture, but provided also for special activity in the realm of social and spiritual life.

It will be observed that from the very beginning the Methodist Episcopal Church has favored a *denominational* organization for her young people rather than the undenominational or interdenominational form now so popular in some quarters. She has all along emphasized certain doctrines and methods which have distinguished her from all sister denominations. We have not imitated others in our theology, hymnology, polity, or methods of practical work. We have always been a peculiar people. "If our fathers had sought to follow other Churches," says Dr. J. L. Hurlbut in a recent admirable discussion of this question, "if they had sought to assimilate with other Churches, to tone down their enthusiasm to the level of others, Methodism would not be in the forefront of progress. The young David of a century ago won his victory, not in Saul's armor, but with weapons all his own. For a hundred years we have been successful according to the measure that we have sought to be ourselves and to do our work in our own way. In dealing with its young people our Church will bring to pass the best results by holding fast to its own traditions while it seeks cordiality and fraternity, but not union of organization, with its sister Churches. The relation of the Church and its young people is too vital for us to hand their supervision over to any outside authority."

The Methodist Episcopal Church is a connectional organization. Plans suited to a denomination having a congregational form of government would not answer our purpose at all. The Epworth League is a vital part of our connectional life, just as are the love feast, the Quarterly Conference, or the Missionary Society. No young people's society officered by persons outside the Church, furnishing literature other than that published by our Book Concern, and conducted upon independent principles could be made permanently operative in Methodism. We must have something in exact harmony with the closely organized and far-reaching activities of our own Church.

It should also be remembered that the working plans of the Epworth League are original. We have borrowed nothing. Every essential feature of our organization has been familiar to Methodism for generations. Is it the consecration service ? Behold the Methodist class meeting for a hundred years. Is it the pledge ? Turn the pages of our history and read of the numerous instances where John Wesley solemnly pledged his earliest members to certain specified duties. Listen also to the testimony of our ministers who have formally pledged their young people to loyalty and service. Is it the appointment of committees to do certain definite churchly duties? Read our book of Discipline from the beginning and you will see that practically the very methods of doing the Lord's great work have been in use for a century as are now so popular and effective in the Epworth League. The League has been an evolution. It has grown from within. We have been conservative in the retention of old methods and progressive in modernizing and adapting them to present-day conditions. These methods are proving effective to a remarkable degree. Yet we do not claim perfection. As new conditions arise new adjustments must be made. What we aim to do is to revive the evangelistic fire and constructive power of primitive Methodism and use them to uplift the teeming thousands who are within the influence of our denomination in these busy times.

But should there not be fraternal cooperation between the young Christian workers of the various denominations? Indeed there should. The historic attitude of the Methodist Church is one of cordial fraternity and practical cooperation with other Churches. We rejoice greatly in their prosperity, and gladly aid them in achieving grander churchly victories. But we are clear in the conviction that the cause of religion can be most effectively advanced by each Church working in its own sphere and by the use of machinery with which it has become familiar. Hence we have never taken very kindly to the almost innumerable "union" projects which have from time to time been started. The Epworth League takes its stand beside its mother in its attitude toward its denominational sisters. To one and

all we sincerely say, " All hail ! "   But we are confident
that greater good can be accomplished when the young
people of each denomination are organized into a society
of their own, said society being an organic part of the
denomination itself. We have denominational Churches.
We have denominational Sunday schools. Why not
denominational young people's societies ? The Churches
and Sunday schools of various denominations work together in the same community in most delightful harmony.   Why should not denominational young people's
societies do so ?   Loyalty to one's own Church need not
subtract sympathy from sincere workers in all other
Churches.   Why should our devotion to the League pre-
vent the most ardent love for our colaborers in the
other splendid young people's organizations ? We are
brethren.   In the golden words of our sainted Simpson, " We live to make our own Church a power in the
land, while we live to love every other Church that exalts our Christ."

CHAPTER II.

THE FIVE ORIGINAL SOCIETIES.

I. THE YOUNG PEOPLE'S METHODIST ALLIANCE.

THE Epworth League is the resultant of the amalgamation of five vital forces—the Young People's Methodist Alliance, the Oxford League, the Young People's Christian League, the Methodist Young People's Union, and the Young People's Methodist Episcopal Alliance. Of these the oldest was the Young People's Methodist Alliance. It came into existence August 25, 1883. Its birthplace was a woody grove on the old and historic Desplaines camp ground, not far from the city of Chicago. The story of its beginning is easily told. Dr. and Mrs. Asbury Lowrey, of New York, visited the camp and preached the Wesleyan doctrine of entire sanctification until hundreds in attendance became greatly interested. Many young people sought a fuller baptism of the Holy Spirit, and a more complete consecration of all for all. The light came clearly. Prejudices melted. Hunger and thirst increased. The filling time came. One day two young women, Misses Winnie S. Benjamin and Lillian E. Date, met by appointment under a certain tree for prayer and conversation. The next day a larger group strolled off to the sequestered spot for conference and prayer. The circle widened until, on August 21,

REPRESENTATIVES OF THE YOUNG PEOPLE'S METHODIST ALLIANCE.

HENRY DATE,   WILLIE W. COOPER,   REV. W. L. COGSHALL,
REV. S. A. KEEN,   REV. S. W. HEALD.   REV. M. D. CARREL.

there were twenty young people in attendance. Rev. John E. Farmer, then a student at the Garrett Biblical Institute, and now a prominent pastor in the Wisconsin Conference, led the service. No language can express the glow of that hour. The little group of twenty were about to wend their way back to camp to attend the afternoon preaching service, when Mr. Frank McCluney, then a young Chicago bookkeeper, and now the pastor of a Methodist Episcopal Church in Florida, proposed that all should at once sign a common covenant. This was well received. Mr. Henry Date, who has since become prominent in evangelistic work, then proposed a permanent young people's society that should aim to keep alive and spread the holy enthusiasm of the hour.

In the mind of Mr. Date the plan was simply for a fraternity whose members should watch and help each the other during the interim between the summer meetings. A committee was appointed to draft a constitution for the coming society, and with a doxology that rang down the woody glen the service ended. Four days later, in the Evanston church cottage the Alliance came into existence with a membership of nearly thirty. This number increased to eighty before the camp meeting closed. The officers elected were: President, Henry Date; Vice President, Rev. John E. Farmer; Corresponding Secretary, Frank McCluney; Recording Secretary, Miss Ida M. Harvey; Treasurer, Miss Minnie Sass; Advisory Committee, Rev. Luke Hitchcock, D.D., Rev. S. M. Davis, D.D., Rev. Frank M. Bristol, D.D.

In August, 1885, the constitution was remodeled and made national in its scope. Provision was made for a monthly paper, a special course of reading, a daily study

2

of the Bible, and the formation of local Alliances in the churches. Up to this time the society was known as the Young People's Christian Alliance, and was only distinctively Methodistic because of the place of its birth and the manner of its life. In November of this year *The Alliance Herald* was launched and at once met with favor. It was the aim of the growing movement to promote loyal cooperation with pastors, daily study of the Bible, avoidance of questionable amusements, holy living and thoughtful enthusiasm, and to lend a hand in keeping the young people in close sympathy with the usages, sacrifices, and experiences that had made the last century of Methodism mighty for God. The standard lifted was as high as that required of a candidate for ministerial orders. All active members were required to sign a pledge, which read:

I enjoy or will seek the blessing of heart purity as taught in the Scriptures. I promise to abstain from the use of tobacco and of all intoxicants as a beverage, to refrain from card-playing and dancing, and from attending the theater, the opera, the circus, and all other questionable places of amusement. I agree to have stated seasons of private prayer, to pray for my pastor and for the members of the Young People's Methodist Alliance, to study the Bible each day, and to give daily thought to the winning of souls, by personal conversation, letter writing, tract distribution, prayer, or other means.

This pledge was not required of associate members. Three mottoes were in use: 1. "Holiness to the Lord." —*Bible.* 2. "We live to make our own Church a power in the land, while we live to love every other Church that exalts our Christ."—*Bishop Simpson.* 3. "All for Jesus."—*Mary D. James.* The badge everywhere worn was a narrow white ribbon with scarlet thread. These ribbons were put on when the pledge was signed, and were the insignia of a consecration made and a covenant taken.

In the fall of 1886 several districts and camp meetings adopted the Alliance, increasing the membership to one thousand. December 1, 1887, there were fifty local societies and over two thousand names on the roll. Far and wide, even into foreign climes, the movement had spread. Men of note not a few spoke words of encouragement. Two conferences were held with Dr. J. H. Vincent, who, in the name of the Oxford League, proposed a uniting of interests. Failing to agree upon a basis of union, the matter was postponed for a season. The genial founder of the Oxford League aided with pen and purse, and often sent words of cheer and encouragement. During the first six months of 1888 the membership again doubled. In July and August summer training schools for Christian workers were held at Crystal Springs, Mich., and at Long Beach, Cal. The first international convention of Methodist young people the world ever saw was held under the auspices of the Alliance at Chicago, in September. Bishops J. M. Walden and William Taylor and Drs. J. L. Hurlbut, C. C. McCabe, J. O. Peck, Hugh Johnston, and other noted men made addresses. In the nine months that followed three hundred new societies were enrolled. It was estimated that over one thousand persons were converted in meetings held. Two men were now kept busy in the field. More than a hundred thousand circulars were quickly distributed. The average monthly expenditure was in excess of four hundred dollars. Mr. Willis W. Cooper, of St. Joseph, Mich., corresponding

secretary, gave the cause much valuable time and toil.
By special request Bishop Merrill appointed Rev. M.
D. Carrel, of the Michigan Conference, superintendent
of the growing interest. The conventions and training
schools held by him in different parts of the country
gave spiritual stimulus to multitudes of young people.

But there were now four other general young people's
societies in Methodism. Each was pushing ahead.
The needs of the hour and the interests of the Church
demanded concentration. Remembering that the Oxford League in the past had wooed wisely but not successfully, the Alliance now made bold to think that
it should spring the question of union. Billets, fragrant
with the perfume of love and sweet fraternity, were
written and sent. Time flew on apace. From all of
the interested parties came responses. The trysting time
came when May blossoms bloomed. What then hap-
pened is now well known.

At its national convention, held at Indianapolis,
July 5, 1889, the Young People's Methodist Alliance indorsed the action of the Cleveland Conference, adopted
the constitution of the Epworth League, and voted itself
out of existence. It was while on the crest-wave of success, with four hundred and ten local societies and nearly
seventeen thousand members, that identity was lost by
a voluntary act, and proof was given that love for the
Church was supreme.

II. THE OXFORD LEAGUE.

The prime mover in the organization and development of the Oxford League was Dr. John H. Vincent.
The General Conference of 1876 made provision for the

Lyceum, but it was found that the purpose of this organization did not meet the needs of the young people. Dr. Vincent, keenly alive to the real requirements of the multitude of young Methodists, sought to supply the vital thing which the Lyceum lacked. He proposed to organize a young people's society that should provide for symmetrical spiritual and intellectual culture. This society was called "The Oxford League," after the famous English university in which the "Holy Club" was founded.

The new organization was received with favor by many pastors and leading laymen, and was given hearty and significant indorsement at the centennial anniversary of the Christmas Conference which was held in Baltimore December 9–17, 1884. The Oxford League, as adopted by this representative body, had for its objects:

I. The commemoration of the meetings of certain students at Oxford, England, between 1729 and 1737, principally under the leadership of John and Charles Wesley, from which meetings were developed the great religious awakenings and revivals of the last century, by which the doctrine and spirit of the Apostolic Church were again given in their fullness to the world and the power of the primitive Church once more established.

II. The furtherance of the fourfold objects of the original Oxford Club: 1. The more careful and devout study of the Holy Scriptures ; 2. The cultivation of a nobler and purer personal Christian character ; 3. The study of the Christian classics for literary culture ; 4. The devising of methods of doing good to others.

The Oxford League aimed, in the fuller development of this scheme, to encourage Methodist youth, 1. To study the Holy Scriptures with a view to the promotion of personal piety ; 2. To become familiar with the Bible origin of the doctrines, spirit, and methods which characterize their own Church ; 3. To trace the presence and development of the Methodistic force in the Holy Catholic Church, from the days of the apostles to the present time ; 4. To trace the origin of the modern, evangelical, and apostolic revival, known as " Methodism "—" Christianity in earnest "—in the rectory of Epworth, the halls of Oxford, and in the consecrated homes of the best English society, and to promote a just appreciation of the strength, scholarship, and dignity of the Methodistic movement ; 5. To promote personal consecration to practical work, carrying the Gospel in personal service to the most needy and the most degraded, to the godless poor and to the godless rich, reading to the bedridden and the blind, visiting the sick room, the hospital, and the prison, looking after new families coming into the community, and inviting children and adults to the Sunday school and the public service, studying the various benevolences of the Church, and thus cultivating intelligent enthusiasm in the entire work of the Church ; 6. To promote intellectual training under the auspices of the Church through church lyceums or other church organizations, especially among those who no longer attend school, and thus develop a rational and refined Christian social life, in which accomplished people may find inspiration and people of limited opportunities be brought into gentle and ennobling and sanctifying fellowship, and thus practically indorse the official deliverances of all Christian Churches in their councils, conventions, conferences, and assemblies against irrational and hurtful amusements ; 7. To further these various ends by the publication and circulation of the permanent documents devoted to the history, philosophy, doctrines, institutions, and achievements of Methodism.

When some one asked Dr. Vincent, " Is it not going backward to set up the Oxford brotherhood of one hundred and fifty years ago as our standard in these times ? " he replied, " The four things they arrived at are the four things we should aim at. In fact, there is no higher idea conceivable than that embraced in the four objects of the old Oxford Club—more Bible knowledge, more literary culture, more personal piety, more practical service. No, we are not going backward in lifting up and seeking their standard."

The Oxford League was denominational — a thoroughly Methodistic movement designed to build up Methodism that Methodism may do more effective work in building up the cause of Christ everywhere. It had no sympathy with the cry for a "crucified denominationalism." Accordingly it met with hostility. In reply to these strictures it answered in the person of its founder : "We must sometimes assert our own position in such a way as to place ourselves diametrically opposite to some of the rest, as when we insist upon the legitimacy of our ministry and repudiate the doctrine of apostolic succession ; but such insistence may be made in the spirit of love. We can avoid sharpness and severity, but we are cowards when we conceal our convictions lest we hurt somebody. Let us hold the truth in love. This will keep us from the ' weak knee ' and the ' cold heart '—two very bad things in any man or Church. We are Christians, Methodist Episcopal Christians. Let us stand there and exert a sweet, persuasive, convincing influence over others."

The character of the Lyceum, the name Oxford, and the possible influence of the Chautauqua movement combined to produce the impression that the Oxford League was designed chiefly for literary and social culture. This was altogether erroneous. The League was specifically religious in its aim. It proposed to promote spiritual life by more Bible study, to broaden the Christian's horizon by a larger culture in the world of thought and expression, and to deepen vital piety by devotional services and tender ministry in Christly work. Alike avoiding mysticism, cant, and one-sided culture, it steadfastly strove for the symmetrical devel-

opment of the whole man. Into this holy service were
pressed all things—pleasant companionships, good libraries, all true social fellowship, all legitimate enjoyment,
all communion with God in nature and God in revelation. In a word, the Oxford League claimed the consecration of every faculty and every opportunity to the
service of Christ.

The success of the movement in the first years was
not extraordinary. Probably the times were not ripe,
and the organization was poorly understood. Still,
a lofty standard was thus lifted and inspiration thus
given to the Church for a forward movement. Numerous chapters were established, and the numbers slowly
increased until the winter of 1889, when the Board of
Control revised somewhat the plans of the League. The
" wheel " devised by Mr. B. E. Helman to set forth the
methods of work and the form of organization for the
local chapter embraced the recent modifications and
attracted general attention. A vigorous policy was inaugurated by Dr. Hurlbut, Secretary of the Sunday
School Union and Tract Society, and the League moved
forward with the tread of a young giant. About five
hundred chapters were enrolled in sixty days, when, lo !
the hour of midnight struck at Cleveland, May 15, 1889,
the Epworth League was born, and the Oxford League
folded its banner and loyally laid its pledges of fealty and
devotion at the feet of this latest born child of promise.

III. THE YOUNG PEOPLE'S CHRISTIAN LEAGUE.

The late Rev. Dr. J. H. Twombly was the origi-
nator of the Young People's Christian League. Rev.
W. I. Haven, who knew Dr. Twombly well, has said of

REPRESENTATIVES OF THE YOUNG PEOPLE'S CHRISTIAN LEAGUE.

REV. WILLIS F. ODELL.   REV. WILLIAM I. HAVEN.   REV. CHARLES A. LITTLEFIELD.

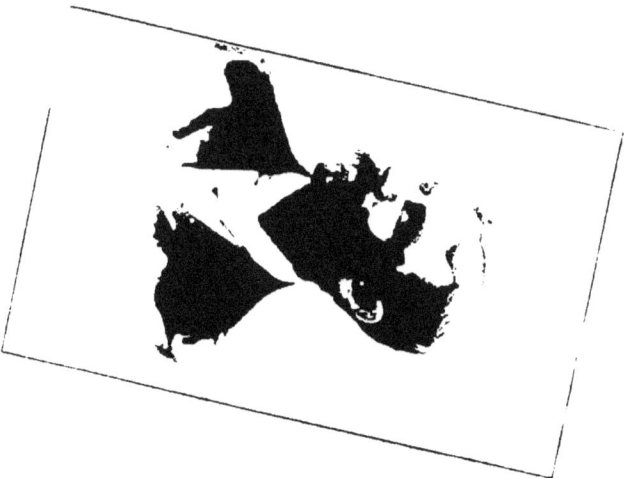

him : "Anyone visiting the New England Conference for the first time might think Dr. Twombly was one of the older members, but they never would make that mistake a second time. His brain is as fertile as that land of promise where 'the plowman overtakes the reaper, and the treader of grapes him that soweth seed.' He never rests in his planning for the interests of the Church. Years ago in his early pastorates he organized the young people for service, and once, as a member of the General Conference, initiated a movement for which the Church is but just ready, so long does it take the rest of the country to see the light that shines on these eastern shores. One of his dreams has been the gathering of a great Methodist international meeting of young people. The hour of the fulfillment of his dream is not far off."

Early in 1887 Dr. Twombly presented a resolution to the Boston Methodist preachers' meeting concerning the welfare of the young people of Methodism, and calling for a convention of the young Methodists of New England. In obedience to this resolution a mass convention was held in Bromfield Street Church, Boston, March 3. The church was crowded morning, afternoon, and evening. Some of the old saints, who have since passed on to the other shore, wept for joy as they saw the sight. At this meeting a committee was appointed to consider the needs of the young people and to call a second convention and report plans for organization and work.

The second convention was held in First Church, Boston, October 26, 1887. It was very important on account of what it prophesied as well as for what it actually accomplished. About three hundred and fifty

young people were present, representing about one
hundred New England churches. Dr. Twombly, the
prime mover in the enterprise, was there. Hon. J. F.
Almy presided at the morning session. Rev. W. P.
Odell, the secretary, read reports from various young
people's societies of New England, whose names were
as numerous as the organizations themselves. This fact
showed very plainly the need of some such movement as
the projectors of the convention contemplated. At this
session Rev. J. M. Durrell read a timely paper on "The
Relation of the Church to the Young People." During the
afternoon session, at which Avery L. Rand, Esq., presided,
a constitution was presented and adopted. The name
"Young People's Christian League" was chosen for
the new organization. The officers elected were: Presi-
dent, Rev. W. I. Haven; Vice Presidents, Rev. J. M.
Durrell, W. H. Thompson, Mrs. H. M. Willard, E. T.
Burrows ; Corresponding Secretary, Rev. W. P. Odell ;
Recording Secretary, Mrs. G. F. Washburn ; Treasurer,
W. M. Flanders ; Auditor, W. S. Allen ; Directors,
Hon. Jacob Sleeper, George H. Van Norman, H. D.
Barber, Mrs. J. W. Barber, Rev. J. D. Pickles, Charles
E. Rice, Rev. J. H. Twombly, D.D., G. C. King,
William Rushton, Mrs. George A. Bates, Miss Isabella
Twombly, and L. E. Hitchcock. During the meeting
Bishop Vincent appeared unexpectedly and was invited
to speak. He suggested as a motto for the League,
"Look up and lift up." This was enthusiastically
adopted. The badge was the same as the present Ep-
worth League badge, except that the letters "Y," "P,"
"C," "L"—Young People's Christian League—appeared
in the arms of the outer cross.

The Young People's Christian League was started with broader plans than any society then existing in the Church. The Young People's Methodist Alliance at that time had only one class of members, and the Oxford League required a uniform constitution, and neither of these societies was able to group together the already existing societies which were in many of our churches. The Young People's Christian League aimed to unify the interests of these older societies, lyceums, guilds, bands, etc., with their local histories and associations, by making them auxiliary to a central body without requiring any change of name or constitution or method of work, wherever these were acceptable to their local church. It was a sort of roundhouse into which different engines might run and get acquainted with each other's whistles in conventions and the like.

Very soon it turned out that there were a good many churches without any societies; so a committee prepared some suggestions for a constitution for such societies. Rev. W. I. Haven says: "We didn't dare do anything but offer suggestions, for here in Yankeeland every group of young people had their own notions about constitutions. We simply required allegiance to their local church to secure relation to the central body, and not uniformity of organization." The organization was very democratic, the officers and board of management being chosen by the delegates from the auxiliaries present in annual convention. Dr. Twombly, in framing the constitution, was very careful to have a door open so that other Methodisms might have a share in the government of the League. Under the efficient oversight of the general secretary, Rev. W. P. Odell, the League grew rapidly. Dr. Parkhurst opened the columns of *Zion's Herald* and helped the cause generously. *Our Youth* also gave up a portion of its columns to the League. The winds bore the seed all over the country until there were auxiliaries in Texas, Dakota, South Carolina, Georgia, New York, Ohio, and many other States outside of New England as well as in all of the New England States. There were also several auxiliaries in the Methodist Episcopal Church, South.

The first annual meeting was held in Tremont Street Church, Boston, October 17, 1888. There were over two hundred delegates present, and the corresponding secretary reported one hundred and seventy-five societies, with a membership of eight thousand. The achievements of the Christian League during its brief career were inspiring, if not numerous. It published and scattered broadcast an Easter letter. It sent a call to all its members in New Hampshire to help in the constitutional amendment campaign. It took part as a body in a similar campaign in Massachusetts. It published leaflets and songs written by its members, and did what it could to bring about the Cleveland Conference and the unification of interests in the Epworth League. Its motto was placed on its badge, and now surrounds the Roman cross of the Epworth League badge. With its devotional, denominational, literary and social, visitation, temperance, mission, and finance departments it attempted to carry out the spirit of its motto, "Look up and lift up." It prepared a reading course and published prayer meeting topics, and by the help of the generous donations of life members paid all its bills. The meetings of the Board of Management

REPRESENTATIVES OF THE METHODIST YOUNG PEOPLE'S UNION.

REV. FREDERICK A. SMART.   REV. C. R. SPENCER.   REV. C. H. MORGAN.
REV. JAMES E. JACKLIN.   REV. SAMUEL PLANTZ.   REV. W. W. WASHBURN.

were held in that "Jerusalem chamber," the trustees' room of Boston University, and deeply interesting sessions they were. The ladies were in its general conferences to start with, and the divine favor was not withheld. Before the second annual meeting the banns were published for the union arranged at Cleveland. Rev. W. I. Haven, Rev. W. P. Odell, and Rev. C. A. Littlefield were present as best men for one of the high contracting parties, and soon the work of the Young People's Christian League as a separate organization was over.

IV. THE METHODIST YOUNG PEOPLE'S UNION.

The Union had its headquarters in Michigan. The organization was the outcome of a meeting of certain alert Detroit Conference pastors. For some time they had been impressed that the time had come for the formation of a society for the social and religious culture of their young people—a society better fitted for this high purpose than any of those already in existence. The matter was first broached in November, 1887, at a session of the Detroit Methodist ministers' meeting. Dr. W. W. Washburn delivered an able address on the subject of young people's societies, after which a committee was appointed to consider the propriety of calling a convention. This committee was composed of Revs. W. W. Washburn, C. M. Cobern, F. A. Smart, and Messrs. John Hall and Frank Bethell. It convened on December 1, 1887. Dr. L. P. Davis, then a pastor in Detroit, was present as an advisory member. The entire question was carefully considered. Finally it was decided to recommend the holding of "a convention to

discuss methods and means to advance the interests of
young people's work in connection with our churches
in the Detroit Conference."

This action was promptly approved by the aforesaid
preachers' meeting. A call was issued, and the convention assembled on December 19 and 20, 1887, in
Central Methodist Episcopal Church, Detroit, Mich.
Delegates from more than fifty churches and young
people's societies attended, and the following topics
were discussed: 1. Necessity of young people's church
societies, and objects to be secured by them. 2. Most
efficient means of securing these objects. 3. Desirabil-
ity of greater uniformity of object and method in our
young people's work.

As a result of the convention a Conference organization was formed, known as the " Young People's Society
of Detroit Conference." A comprehensive constitution
was adopted. Many of its best features were ultimately incorporated in the plan of the Epworth League.
Hon. Horace Hitchcock, of Detroit, was the first president, and Rev. Frederick A. Smart the secretary. The
movement spread with great rapidity. Soon its fame
was widely "noised abroad." Inquiries for the model
constitution were received from nearly every State in
the Union and from foreign parts. One year of trial
and success convinced the managers of the society that
there was something in the movement worth giving to
the world. Consequently, at the annual meeting held
in the Jefferson Street Methodist Episcopal Church,
Saginaw, Mich., December 4, 1888, the constitution was
so revised as to provide for a more general organization,
under the name "Methodist Young People's Union."

At this meeting communications were received from Rev. W. I. Haven, President of the Young People's Christian League, and Rev. M. D. Carrel, Superintendent of the Young People's Methodist Alliance, each urging union with his respective society. But the managers were seeking a larger union, and felt that the way to secure it most speedily was to "force the fighting" for their ideas. So the Union was launched. Rev. W. W. Washburn, D.D., was elected president, and Rev. Frederick A. Smart corresponding secretary. Provision was made for the publication of *Our Young People*, a monthly paper for young Methodists, under the joint editorial management of Revs. C. B. Spencer and P. Ross Parrish. Only two numbers of this periodical appeared, since it was shortly after merged into *Our Youth*, the provisional organ of the Epworth League. The amended model constitution was now mailed broadcast, and the society bade fair to become as numerous in membership as competing organizations. The spirit of the "Union" management was evidenced in this article by the corresponding secretary, which appeared in the columns of the *Michigan Christian Advocate*. The reasons for reorganization are as follows:

1. The success of our form of organization in the first year of its existence, and the constant demand for information concerning our methods and purpose from all sections of the country, which proves that many workers in this inviting field are still looking for the *ne plus ultra* in young people's societies.

2. We believe that the theory of our movement is unassailable, and the statement of that theory in our new constitution, soon to be printed, nearly perfect.

3. Those interested have been close students of the plans, methods, and work of all other organizations of similar nature, and find

nearly all of them lacking in some feature deemed by us important.

4. It seems desirable that all such societies everywhere, holding our views of the need of the work, should enter into closer fellowship, with more adequate means of intercommunication than we have yet enjoyed.

In order to serve these ends our society has taken the name "Methodist Young People's Union" of the Methodist Episcopal Church. We have overleaped the Conference boundary and formed a general organization for the whole Church. We are fairly in the field, and challenge brotherly emulation on the part of contemporary organizations, believing that in such a friendly and Christian competition the true policy will be developed. In the domain of literary achievements we desire to be excelled by none; in the development of the social nature we do not expect to be outdone, and in spiritual things we hang our banner on the outer walls, inscribed "Holiness unto the Lord." Our literature, which will soon be issued, will outline more fully our plans; our organ, christened *Our Young People*, will keep these plans before the Church, and our reliance for success is on the Holy Spirit.

With such a spirit manifested by the active management of the various societies, no great length of time could elapse without consolidation. Upon the issuance of the call for the Cleveland Conference the Union promptly appointed the following delegates: Revs. W. W. Washburn, D.D., F. A. Smart, C. B. Spencer, C. H. Morgan, Samuel Plantz, and J. E. Jacklin. This delegation participated earnestly in the discussions of the Conference. They went there with an ardent desire for union and well-prepared plans to bring it about. No body of men were more alert, conscientious, and influential in the memorable two days' conference, and none rejoiced more sincerely over the happy outcome.

REPRESENTATIVES OF THE NORTH OHIO CONFERENCE METHODIST
EPISCOPAL ALLIANCE.

REV. ORLANDO BADGLEY.	REV. J. S. REAGER.	REV. L. J. HOADLEY.
REV. G. A. REEDER, JR.	REV. L. K. WARNER.	REV. P. J. MILLS.

V. THE NORTH OHIO CONFERENCE METHODIST EPISCO-
PAL ALLIANCE.

The fifth of the "original societies" was but an infant
when the consolidation took place. The organizers
doubtless hoped that they had found the solution of the
problem that was vexing the leaders of the younger
hosts of Methodism. One who was high in the councils
of this new organization has said that the North Ohio
Conference Methodist Episcopal Alliance was the out-
growth of a desire for the consolidation of all Methodist
Episcopal societies of young people into one great connectional society. The want of such a society had long
been felt among the pastors of the North Ohio Conference, within whose bounds chapters of the Young
People's Methodist Alliance, Oxford League, and Christian League had been established. At the session of
the Conference held at Ashland, O., in September, 1888,
an Oxford League committee was appointed for the
purpose of considering certain matters pertaining to
young people's societies which had been presented to
the Conference. This committee was made up of Revs.
W. A. Robinson, E. O. Buxton, B. J. Hoadley, G. W.
Huddleston, J. S. Reager, E. Persons, R. T. Stevenson,
H. L. Steves, and C. A. Wustenberg. The committee
presented the following resolution, the unanimous adoption of which was an index to the sentiment of the body:

Resolved, That we believe a great connectional young people's
organization that would enlist the cooperation of all our Conferences
would tend to the greatest improvement in intelligence, piety, and
methods of Christian work. In view of the existence of two or
three Methodist societies, having for their object the accomplish-
3

ment of the same purpose, your committee would recommend that efforts be made to secure the consolidation of all these societies into one. We also recommend the appointment of Rev. J. S. Reager, of this Conference, as Conference secretary for the purpose of securing such consolidation, and for the distribution of information upon this subject among our charges.

In harmony with this action of the Conference the presiding elders appointed district secretaries as follows: Rev. F. G. McCauley, Mount Vernon District; Rev. L. K. Warner, Wooster District; Rev. G. A. Reeder and Rev. Austin Philpott, Mansfield District; Rev. O. Badgley, Galion District; Rev. B. J. Mills, Sandusky District. A meeting of the secretaries—Conference and district—was held at Mansfield, O., December 6, 1888. It was held in the study of Rev. N. S. Albright, who assisted the secretaries in the formation of a plan of organization and in drafting a constitution. This work engaged the secretaries for two days. The result of their work was accepted generally by the pastors of the Conference, and the organization of local societies was pushed with energy. Before the close of the winter the districts were all organized and new societies were rapidly multiplying on the charges.

While these brethren in Ohio were pushing their society with vigor, feeling confident that they were doing their share toward the creation of the ultimate society, the invitation was received to attend the convention that had been called to meet at Cleveland May 14, 1889. With the assurance that there was a strong providential element in this new venture, the North Ohio Conference Alliance sent Revs. J. S. Reager, L. K. Warner, G. A. Reeder, Jr., O. Badgley, B. J. Mills, and

B. J. Hoadley to Cleveland as its representatives. These brethren took an active part in the deliberations of that historic gathering, and rejoiced over the results. An enthusiastic convention was held at Shelby, O., May 28, 1889. The convention was composed of delegates from the local societies of the North Ohio Conference Alliance, by whom the heartiest indorsement was given to the action of the Cleveland Conference, and the new name of Epworth League was unanimously adopted.

CHAPTER III.

THE BIRTH OF THE EPWORTH LEAGUE.

THERE are certain localities of historic interest to which Methodists instinctively turn with gratitude and pride. Epworth, the home of the Wesley family, is one of them. City Road Chapel, in London, is another. Old John Street Church, in New York city, is still another. Others are old St. George's Church, in Philadelphia, and Lovely Lane Chapel, in Baltimore. Future ,historians of Methodism will need to place Cleveland, O., in their list of favored names, for in that city the Epworth League was born. The event occurred on the 15th of May, 1889, in the Central Methodist Episcopal Church. The old building in which the historic meeting was held has been removed, and a handsome modern structure, known as the Epworth Memorial Church, has taken its place.

As we have indicated in a previous chapter, negotiations had been carried on for some weeks between representatives of the five general young people's societies of our Church looking toward a possible union. That some steps ought to be taken to centralize and harmonize the work was freely admitted. But just what method would most easily and successfully bring about the desired consummation was a question not easily answered. Finally the leaders of the Young People's Methodist Alliance proposed a conference. This plan

CENTRAL METHODIST EPISCOPAL CHURCH, CLEVELAND, O.

met with favor.   In due time an invitation was extended
by Rev. B. F. Dimmick, pastor of the Central Church,
Cleveland, to representatives of the various societies to
meet in that edifice.   The invitation was accepted.   On
the morning of Tuesday, May 14, the leaders met face to
face.   As the personnel of the Cleveland Conference will
always be a matter of peculiar interest the names are
here recorded.

The Young People's Methodist Alliance was represented by Rev. Henry Date, a Chicago Methodist local
preacher and successful evangelist; Rev. M. D. Carrel,
now a valued *attaché* of the Western Methodist Book
Concern at Cincinnati ; Rev. Dr. S. A. Keen, the soul-
winning evangelist ; Dr. S. W. Heald, Secretary of the
Upper Iowa Conference ; Dr. W. I. Cogshall, now Presiding Elder of the Grand Rapids District, Mich., and
Mr. Willis W. Cooper, a manufacturer of St. Joseph,
Mich., who has for years been widely known as a consecrated and successful Christian worker.

The Oxford League had as its representatives Rev.
Dr. J. L. Hurlbut, Corresponding Secretary of the Sun-
day School Union and Tract Society; Rev. Dr. J. M.
Freeman, Assistant Corresponding Secretary of the
Sunday School Union and Tract Society; Dr. R. R.
Doherty, Recording Secretary of the same ; Rev. Dr. J.
Embury Price, a prominent New York city pastor ;
Rev. James T. Docking, now a pastor in the New Eng-
land Southern Conference, and Mr. Bryon E. Helman,
a successful merchant and prominent Methodist of
Cleveland, O.   The Oxford League also had reserve
delegates, as follows : Rev. J. C. W. Coxe, D.D., of
Iowa ; Rev. A. H. Gillet, D.D., Cincinnati ; Rev. J. W.

Kennedy, of Michigan, and Mr. W. M. Day, of Cleveland, O.

The Christian League sent Rev. William I. Haven, of Boston, known and loved throughout Methodism; Rev. Willis P. Odell, then of New England Conference, but now pastor of Delaware Avenue Church, Buffalo, N. Y., and Rev. C. A. Littlefield, at present pastor of Asbury Church, Springfield, Mass.

The Methodist Young People's Union commissioned a full delegation as follows: Rev. Dr. W. W. Washburn, of Saginaw; Rev. Charles H. Morgan, now of Howell; Rev. Samuel Plantz, of Tabernacle Church, Detroit; Rev. Frederick A. Smart, at present successfully engaged in promoting the financial interests of Albion College; Rev. James E. Jacklin, for the past three years Associate Editor of the *Michigan Christian Advocate;* and Rev. Claudius B. Spencer, the popular pastor of Christ Church, Denver, Colo. ·

The Alliance of the North Ohio Conference was honored with this able representation : Rev. J. S. Reager, Rev. G. A. Reeder, Jr., Rev. B. J. Mills, Rev. B. J. Hoadley, Rev. Orlando Badgley, and Rev. L. K. Warner. These brethren were then all influential pastors in the North Ohio Conference, and, with one exception, we believe, they are still toiling in that field.

The Conference was called to order by Mr. Willis W. Cooper. A hymn was sung, and Dr. Hurlbut led in prayer. Mr. Cooper was then chosen temporary chairman, and Dr. A. H. Gillet, recently translated to the heavenly home, was named as temporary secretary. Committees on permanent organization and order of business were appointed. Brothers Doherty, Odell, Cogs-

hall, Smart, and Reeder served on the former, and
Brothers Price, Carrel, Littlefield, Mills, and Morgan
on the latter. Rev. B. F. Dimmick, pastor of the Central Church, was requested to act as Committee on Credentials. The Committee on Permanent Organization
was not long in selecting officers, and upon its nomination Mr. Cooper was elected chairman, and Rev. Claudius
B. Spencer secretary. It was agreed that the voting
be done by delegations, and that each delegation have
a right to six votes.

In order to secure a frank and full expression of opinion from the delegates upon the important problem
which had called them together, it was decided that a
representative of each society should occupy ten minutes, suggesting, if possible, some basis of union. After
a brief recess for consultation Henry Date spoke for the
Methodist Alliance, and nominated the following basis
for the hoped-for consolidation : 1. Uniform constitution. 2. Self-government under a general board, autonomy. 3. A strong spiritual element. The Oxford
League was represented by Robert R. Doherty, its recording secretary. He gave a history of the League
and its " new departure." He was unable, however, as
yet to make suggestions for the proposed union. Rev.
W. I. Haven was spokesman for the Young People's
Christian League. These were his recommendations :
1. Publishing interests centered in New York. 2. General organization centered in New York. 3. General
secretary to be the Corresponding Secretary of the Sunday School Union. 4. General Conference district
organizations, to a large degree autonomous; these districts to each elect two delegates to a convention which

should be held quadrennially at the seat of the General Conference. 5. Local constitutions with pledge, and local constitutions without pledge. 6. A Board of Control, to consist of the delegates from each of the General Conference districts, a number of bishops, and others. Dr. Washburn expressed the wishes of the Young People's Union, and suggested these planks for the union platform : 1. A pledge, but not to be insisted upon from all. 2. A paper. 3. A general organization similar in plan to that outlined by the representative of the Christian League. 4. A strong spiritual element. For the North Ohio Conference delegates Rev. J. S. Reager said they were ready to make any proper concession for union. Thus the morning hours were spent in fraternal exchange of sentiment. Before adjournment it was clear that while the desire for a united society was strong very serious obstacles were in the way of its consummation.

When the brethren came together in the afternoon Rev. W. I. Haven led in prayer, asking most earnestly for divine guidance and help. After a brief conference with his colleagues Dr. Hurlbut made these propositions for a united society: 1. A strong spiritual foundation. 2. A local society to be organized under the authority of the local church. 3. The general organization to be managed by a Board of Control, chosen like the other general officers of the Church, by the General Conference, but upon nomination by the bishops.

All the societies having now submitted a basis of union which they considered fair and equitable, a committee on " Consolidation " was appointed. These are the men who were named : M. D. Carrel, J. E. Price,

W. P. Odell, Samuel Plantz, and L. K. Warner. This committee soon presented a model general Constitution for the consolidated societies. It embraced many of the features of that which eventually became the general Constitution of the Epworth League. The report was laid on the table until the next meeting.

The committee of one from each society which had been appointed during the afternoon to confer about the publication of a newspaper organ now asked permission to report. Its recommendation was that *Our Youth* be modified so as to give more prominence to the religious and social features of the proposed united society. Then the Conference decided to adjourn till the morning.

Wednesday morning, May 15, a day to be forever memorable in the history of Methodism, found the little company of anxious brethren again assembled in the class room of Central Church. A half hour was spent in prayer. What could have been more appropriate? One of the most influential movements in the history of our denomination was about to assume organic form. How important that the Head of the Church should be present to guide and control the deliberations of the Conference upon this historic day!

First in order was the consideration of reports which had been laid upon the table at the previous session. Those on " Consolidation " and " General Organization " were first considered. The discussion was fraternal and free, and, with slight amendments, both the documents were approved. Inasmuch as the general plan formed the basis for the model general Constitution of the Epworth League and will be quoted in full in a subse-

quent chapter, its insertion is not considered essential
here.

The selection of a *name* for the proposed united society awakened much interest. The committee made
this recommendation:

While we agree that the retention of the name of each society
here represented would probably conduce to the strength of that society for the time being, we have felt, nevertheless, that the interests
of the work at large should only be consulted, and that those interests may be best subserved by mutual concession.

We are in practical agreement that we can select no better noun
than *League*. As to the adjective we are not agreed. The majority
of your committee favors *The Wesley League ;* one votes for *The
Oxford League*, and one for *The Christian League*.

We make this tentative report as the completest we can now reach,
and reserve our individual rights on the final vote.

The vote showed that the problem had been pretty
thoroughly discussed by the committee. If these brethren could not agree upon a name after careful and pro-
longed consideration it was hardly to be expected that
the Conference could do so at once. Motions, amendments, and substitutes followed each other in rapid succession. Agreement seemed to be improbable. Finally
it was resolved to go into committee of the whole, and
see if some conclusion could not be reached. But the
hour of adjournment was already at hand, and, after
electing Mr. Cooper chairman, the committee postponed
further consideration till afternoon.

The devotional meeting with which the afternoon session opened will not be soon forgotten by those who
were present. Nearly all the delegates participated.
The attitude of the little company was one of entire
consecration, and their petition was for guidance in the

important steps they were now taking. Then the perplexing question of a name for the proposed society
was again taken up. Remarks were made by almost
every one present. Various suggestions were volun-
teered. Some new combinations of words were proposed.
Finally an informal ballot was agreed to. This was
the result : The Wesley League, twelve votes ; The Epworth League, nine ; The Oxford League, eight ; The
Young People's League of the Methodist Episcopal
Church, one. This vote, it will be remembered, was
taken in the committee of the whole. When it was announced Dr. Hurlbut moved that the committee rise
and report the name " Wesley League " to the Conference. Some of the brethren were eager to substitute
the name " Oxford " for " Wesley." Hence more friendly
discussion was indulged in. But the name " Wesley
League " was adopted by a decisive vote, and the committee so reported to the Conference. In the Conference the debate was resumed. But the name suggested
was ultimately adopted, and " Wesley League " became
temporarily the cognomen of the projected society.

Then followed a careful examination of the report of
the Committee on Local Constitution. Inasmuch as
many of the plans outlined by the committee were not
finally adopted by the Epworth League it is perhaps
hardly necessary to give the document space here. It
may be said in brief, however, that the plan contemplated a society having active and associate membership, with a pledge for each class. The officers were
to consist of a president, a vice president, a secretary, a
treasurer, and the chairmen of standing committees ;
these officers, with the pastor, to form a " Board of

· Managers." The following standing committees were proposed: Devotional, Denominational, Literary, Social Work, Visitation, and Finance. A footnote stated that the pledge for active members was recommended for general adoption; but if in any church this pledge should be found to be an obstacle to the formation of a League the members might adopt the associate members' pledge and sign the Constitution.

The Conference went into a committee of the whole to consider the proposed local Constitution. Time was rapidly slipping away, and for economical reasons all speeches were limited to three minutes each. Messrs. Hurlbut, Keen, Carrel, Warner, Smart, Date, Doherty, Freeman, Washburn, Haven, Morgan, Odell, Docking, and Badgley took part in the animated debate. Pending a decision a recess of ten minutes was taken by request of the representatives of the Oxford League. Upon reassembling this frank and courteous communication was read by Dr. Hurlbut:

DEARLY BELOVED BRETHREN: We, the representatives of the Oxford League, desire to make the following statement:

We do not feel authorized to surrender the organization of the Oxford League as an institution of the Methodist Episcopal Church. During the two months which have elapsed since the " new departure " was entered upon the League, by its various Conference societies, by State conventions, and by its central authorities, has endeavored as rapidly as possible to perfect its organization on a broadly representative principle. Already this development has so far progressed as to secure adequate representation to every local chapter, to give to each a voice in the general government of the League, and to make our Board of Control a large and truly representative body. We will gladly receive from this Conference any suggestions as to modification of plan; we will carefully consider them, and will submit them to the bishops and Board of Control.

"Unification" is still our earnest desire, but under the circumstances it is perhaps better for us not to participate in your further discussions as to the formation of a new society. In our effort to harmonize differences we have proposed to surrender many of the most cherished features of our general management ; we have consented, tentatively, to a surrender of our name, and to make many other concessions. But *we cannot give up our Constitution.* We assure you of our hearty love and our warmest wishes for your success in all Christian endeavor. We will joyfully greet any who elect to join us, and we will at any time gladly meet in convention and conference our brethren of various societies for consultation upon the best plans of work.

The delegates of the Oxford League then withdrew from the room. When the Conference recovered from its surprise a motion was made and carried to spread the communication just received upon the journal. Revs. L. K. Warner and B. J. Mills, of the North Ohio Conference Alliance, asked to be excused from the Conference because of sympathy with the action of the representatives of the Oxford League. The request was granted.

The withdrawal of the delegates of the Oxford League, followed soon after by the two North Ohio brethren, threw the Conference into a state of mind bordering upon consternation. It surely looked as though the object of the meeting was after all to fail of attainment. Several eyewitnesses of the scene describe it as most pathetic. All knew that a momentous crisis had come. So the brethren betook themselves to prayer. One after another talked with God. While they yet asked, the answer came. Everyone felt the divine presence. Rev. W. I. Haven, with the tears rolling down his face, said: "I am willing to concede anything, even the name;

we must not leave this place without securing the end
for which we came—union." All agreed that he was
right. So after a most affecting season of prayer a committee consisting of W. I. Haven, S. A. Keen, J. E.
Jacklin, and Orlando Badgley was appointed to wait
upon the Oxford League delegates and invite them to
return to the Conference. The committee was instructed to say that the Conference was willing to consider the local Constitution of the Oxford League *seria-
tim*, instead of that reported by the special committee of
the Conference.

A recess of ten minutes was taken to await the report
of the committee. After half an hour had been spent in
prayer and testimony, in the continued absence of the
committee, it was agreed to continue the recess subject
to the call of the chairman. Thus came to a close the
afternoon session.

When the brethren filed into the little room for the
evening session there was upon every face a strange
commingling of anxiety and hopefulness. They knew
that the problem would in all probability be solved in
some form before they left the church that night. What
would the solution be? No one could tell. Yet it
was felt that the work in which they were engaged was
of God, and he surely would find a way out of the present embarrassment. It was this confidence that gave
such tenderness and buoyancy to the prayers of
Brothers Keen, Reager, and Jacklin in the opening devotions.

Rev. W. I. Haven reported that his committee had
visited the Oxford League delegates according to instructions, and that Dr. Hurlbut and Dr. Price, who were

present, would report their answer. Dr. Hurlbut read
the following:

DEARLY BELOVED BRETHREN: We have listened to the kind
representations made by Brother W. I. Haven, on behalf of your
committee.

We have already tentatively made as large concessions as we feel
authorized to make, and are convinced that union can be effected at
this stage only on the following basis:

1. That the Oxford League Constitution be accepted as it stands,
with whatever merely verbal changes may be found necessary to
adapt it immediately to the needs of all associations that may affiliate
with it ; but that for all constitutional changes we await the complete
organization of our new Board of Control.

2. That District and Conference Leagues be organized as rapidly
as possible.

3. That modifications and amendments to the Constitution may
be made upon the recommendation of local Leagues through the
regular lines (that is, through district and Conference organizations)
to the Board of Control, for consideration and decision.

4. That the names "Oxford League" and "Wesley League"
be submitted to every local society for choice, and that a majority of
these societies determine the name.

5. The present names of all uniting societies to be used until final
action of the Board of Control.

On behalf of the representatives of the Oxford League,

ROBERT R. DOHERTY, *Secretary.*

This paper was received and carefully considered.
At length Rev. C. A. Littlefield introduced this memorial to the Oxford League delegation:

DEAR BRETHREN OF THE OXFORD LEAGUE : The principles upon
which you agree to form a general organization have been carefully
considered by us, and we have agreed to adopt them, and in connection with them present to you the following propositions, upon
which we will join in a general organization:

1. The name shall be " The Epworth League."

2. The formation of a constitution for local chapters shall be submitted to the Board of Control.

3. Until the Board of Control shall draft and present such a constitution we shall work under the local Constitution of the Oxford League, after it has been verbally amended.

4. The pledge presented to the Conference by our Committee on Local Constitution shall be placed in the By-laws of the Epworth League, with a note stating that its use is optional.

5. The preamble stating the aim of the League reported by the Committee on Local Constitution shall be the statement of the aim of the Epworth League in the amended Constitution.

In a few minutes this memorial was adopted. The Oxford League delegates, feeling that this action left them free to act without violating the instructions of the organization which had commissioned them, resumed their seats in the Conference. Upon formal motion *the union of the five societies was effected.* Smiles lighted up many faces, and tears of gladness and gratitude stood in many eyes. That for which so many had longed and prayed was at last almost an accomplished fact. Was it not enough to thrill every heart with joy?

The local Constitution of the Oxford League was then read, and the modifications suggested by the Conference were noted by Dr. Hurlbut.

Upon motion of Dr. Hurlbut, the white ribbon, with a scarlet thread running through the center from end to end, and which had been adopted as the badge of the Young People's Methodist Alliance, was chosen as the "colors" of the new League. The question of a badge then came up. It was resolved that the Maltese cross, with the initials and motto of the League, should be adopted. The Maltese cross had been used as a badge

both by the Oxford League and the Young People's
Christian League.

Upon motion of Rev. M. D. Carrel, the motto of the
Young People's Christian League was selected as the
motto of the new organization, "Look up; lift up." It
was also agreed that this sentence from John Wesley,
used by the Oxford League as a motto, be adopted as a
sentiment of the Epworth League: "I desire to form a
league, offensive and defensive, with every soldier of
Jesus Christ." The forceful words of Bishop Simpson,
"We live to make our own Church a power in the land,
while we live to love every other Church that exalts our
Christ," were also chosen as a sentiment of the League.

The hour of midnight approached as these final details were arranged. It was a memorable hour. It
would have been difficult to find upon all the earth a
happier company of men. Congratulations over the result of the negotiations were joyfully exchanged. Faces
were illumined by gladness. "Praise God" was an
exclamation which fell in all sincerity from many lips.
Did ever a company of Christians sing the doxology
with more fervor and meaning? Our brethren had a
right to be glad, for they had, under God, laid the
foundations of an institution which was destined to be
one of the mightiest forces in all the history of the
Christian Church.

4

CHAPTER IV.

INCIDENTS AND IMPRESSIONS OF THE CLEVELAND CONFERENCE.

I. BY REV. HENRY DATE, OF THE YOUNG PEOPLE'S METHODIST ALLIANCE.

A BABE cannot be an egotist, therefore it is always in order for a growing child to sit for its picture. Pike's Peak can be easily photographed, because it long ago acquired the habit of standing still. But it takes a sensitive film, a lightning shutter, and a quick-acting lens to sketch the wing of a humming bird in motion. No perfect likeness of the Epworth League will exist until the child calms down, ceases to grow, and exchanges the restlessness of youth for the quiet of old age. While a picture is out of the question, the early impressions of those who first saw the little one and its cradle are in order and of interest.

Before a panorama of the Battle of Gettysburg stood a veteran with an empty coat-sleeve, and beside him stood one who was but a boy when Abraham Lincoln called for troops. At first the men stood silent while memory and art told the story of the conflict. The younger man saw the cannons. The older soldier heard them. One viewed the scene from the eminence of the present. The other retreated down the lane of time one quarter of a century, and lived an age in a single day. "That was a great battle," said the youth. "Yes," replied the veteran, "it was a great battle. I was there." The head lifted ; the eyes sparkled ; the face flushed; the empty sleeve shook. Into three monosyllables the soldier had thrown the greatest chapter in the story of his life.

Four years of to-morrow have sped past to-day and into yesterday since the May morning when twenty-seven soldiers of the Church militiant surrounded a vexed problem, and, after thought, prayer, and praise, surrendered each to the other. The conflict was more of an Appomattox than a Gettysburg. The contestants were not soldiers but peace commissioners. "I was there." You have heard it before. You will hear it again. Well for at least one that he was there, for, had not this "tide in the affairs of men" reached where his craft lay stranded, he would have gone down to the grave a stranger to fame, and without leaving a single footprint on the sands of time. Who of the number will live longest to tell the story ? Who one day will be left alone ? In years to come who will be led "in age and feebleness extreme" to the platform to look into the faces of the youth of the next century to whisper tremblingly, "I was there?" That day will find Methodism a unit, and heaven nearer earth than now.

1. *The Epworth League was launched in a storm.* The United States Weather Bureau put out no danger signal, but on May 14 and 15, 1889, Cleveland was a storm center. The barometer fell ;. the elements warred ; the atmosphere cleared ; the clouds rolled away ; sunshine came. The men who met to knock away the stocks under the crafts to be launched were not lovers

at first sight. All came into the ecumenical shipyard
on probation. No one was at once taken into full connection. "Blest be the tie that binds" was sung, but it
would have required a surgical operation to have found
the tie. A recital of all that transpired during these
two days would fill a book. The novel, if ever written,
will be in six chapters : (1) Met ; (2) Disagreed ; (3)
Parted ; (4) Reflection ; (5) Reconciliation ; (6) Affiliation. The Epworth League is a continued story.
Many chapters are yet to follow. No one can tell how
the tale will end, but it is predicted that the last chapter will reveal the Methodist youth of all lands and
climes clasping hands and marching under one common standard.

The smallest man in the convention made the first
speech. He spoke for the Young People's Methodist
Alliance, and in three minutes outlined the wishes and
the attitude of his associates to the question of union.
The tallest man in the room then arose, and in the
name of the Oxford League watched the clock for five
minutes, while he made the most unique speech of the
day. The speaker started out to go nowhere and
reached his destination. He essayed to say naught and
succeeded. His figures were all ciphers. Like Noah's
dove, he encompassed sea and land, but came home to
those who watched and waited, with no olive branch to
show that *terra firma,* or the main question, had been
touched. But Robert R. Doherty is one of the
brainiest and most genial of men. He is a diplomat,
and those for whom he spoke knew how to play chess.
An Irish patriot, on the threshold of a great speech,
passed a portion of the night before walking the

floor of his room. Some one passing the door heard him pray, "O Lord, on to-morrow teach me what not to say." If a similar prayer ascended from a Pullman sleeping car at midnight on May 13, 1889, it was answered before the noon of the next day. Dr. Hurlbut in the afternoon playfully confessed that the speech of the morning was part of a program, and that now the Oxford League was ready to declare its wishes and intentions. It was willing to play Jonah if it could be the whale. The affiliation at Cleveland was more or less of an absorption, plus a few changes and a new name. Going home from Cleveland to Detroit, one delegate remarked, "Well, boys, we are going home, and have lost all." "No," laughingly replied one in the group, "we still have our half-fare railroad passes."

On the afternoon of the second day the West stood on the threshold of the East and waited. Toward evening the East came to the doorstep of the West and was admitted. Love never runs smoothly where the motives of love are misunderstood. When heart sees heart heads are apt to come together.

2. *The Epworth League was launched by optimists.* Optimism is a faith. Pessimism is doubt. Thomas was a pessimist. Paul was an optimist. Between the two was Pentecost. There is but little virtue in blue glass, and no virtue in blue people. An optimist is one who lives on the sunny side of the street, and whose house is built on the promises of God. The men who met in conference at Cleveland with the eye of faith saw into the future. In no small degree they caught a vision of that which is a fact to-day. Each one felt the importance of the hour, and well knew that future weal or woe

was hanging in the balance of the moment. Henry
Clay on Allegheny heights heard not more distinctly the
footfall of the coming millions than did they.

3. *The Epworth League was launched in a Pentecost.*
The Epworth League was christened by men, but its
baptism was from above. In the beginning it called on
the God of Elijah, and toward evening heaven answered
by fire. Its genesis was a Pentecost. While debate was
earnest and at times heated, faith and prayer were constant. James Caughey was once asked the secret of
his revivals. "Knee work," was his reply. The Epworth League is the product of petition. On the afternoon when the conference divided and fond hopes
seemed blasted the brethren who remained—and for
aught we know those who withdrew—went at once to
their knees for divine guidance. Hearts warmed ; eyes
filled ; spirits quieted ; debate gave way to trust ;
faith took hold, and a conviction that all would be
well came. Again a Methodist classroom was a vesti-
bule to one of the outer courts of heaven. In the
abiding presence of the Holy Spirit is tabernacled hope.
Should he withdraw his presence from the Church her
bush of fire would become a heap of ashes, and her rock
of power the resting place of dry bones.

II. BY REV. JACOB EMBURY PRICE, D.D., OF THE OXFORD
LEAGUE.

OUR first meeting in Cleveland on the morning of
May 15, 1889, brought us together from widely separated points. It soon appeared that, while there would
be a clash and conflict of ideas, here was a company of
earnest Christians and loyal Methodists who were anx-

iously seeking some basis for the unification of our young people's work. Strangers to each other, we quickly realized that we were brethren.

Was there a spirit or method of diplomacy? Yes, in the noblest sense of that much-abused word. We now speak for the Oxford League. We had to do more than defend our convictions. We cherished honestly the view—though it would have given offense to others to assert it strongly—that the Oxford League, indorsed by the Board of Bishops and the Sunday School Union, really had an official standing and an official connection that we could not forget or ignore. By this view of our obligation we were bound and restrained to operate within fixed lines, and, we suppose, were thought to be obstinate.

Our first desire was to get from our brethren just what they wanted, and not to put forward any proposition of our own until compelled to do so; and we were then prepared to concede everything we conscientiously could. Accordingly, Dr. Doherty was asked to speak for us and consume our ten minutes, but to commit us to nothing. This he admirably accomplished, though it is a difficult thing for one whose mind is so fertile with ideas either to speak or to write and say nothing.

In the distribution of the work the writer was assigned to the Committee on Periodicals, and so had to defend in a sturdy way the merits of *Our Youth*, then the organ of the Oxford League. By no means satisfied with that excellent paper as an organ for the new organization, we were persuaded the time was not yet ripe for anything other. We labored with the four other members of the committee until they saw the question in the same light as ourselves and brought in a favorable report. We are still convinced that this action was wise. *The Epworth Herald* is all the better and the more prosperous for the delay until " the fullness of times."

The banquet at the Hollenden on the evening of our arrival was a good preparation for our meeting, and, like all other work done by Cleveland Methodists, was in every way worthy. The convention of Ohio Oxford Leagues also contributed its enthusiasm, though having no direct connection with our gathering. The withdrawal of the Oxford League representatives from the convention on the afternoon of the second day is commonly known. This action may have been regarded as a *coup d'état*. Whatever may be said of it, this much we know. In the proceedings of the first day it became apparent to us that concessions would be asked which we could not conscientiously make. To provide for such a contingency, which our representatives thought inevitable, we prepared a statement, and in the late afternoon of the second day, when the expected crisis had come, we asked for a recess. The paper was then signed and presented to the Convention, and we withdrew. Fortunately, the concessions asked were subsequently modified. We again met, reached a common ground, and then followed a love feast as delightful as any held for a hundred years.

Looking back now, we cannot but feel that we were divinely guided. The Oxford League representatives made very large demands in that they asked for the adoption of the local Constitution of the Oxford League and insisted upon official control through the Board of

Bishops, the Sunday School Union, and the Tract Society. That these demands were very unacceptable to
other societies we can well understand. Still, they conceded them finally, and in a brotherly spirit. Their
action deserves the lasting gratitude of the Church, for
thus they made possible the Epworth League.

On the other hand, we are sure our firmness was mis-
taken for obstinacy, and very naturally so. Our brethren could not feel as we felt the pressure of responsibility arising from what we apprehended as an official
relation. This we could not sacrifice. We felt the
odium that must attach to our course in the eyes of
other representatives, but our duty was plain. We now
believe that in this we too were divinely aided. Official connection was secured for the new organization,
and this was of incalculable advantage in the conflicts
it had to face. At once it was given the right of way—
a priority over other societies. Besides, in its infancy
it had thus secured to it a home and a support. It
was not burdened with financial responsibility. Its expenses were met without embarrassment. For its promotion it must develop and train its own workers and
speakers; and how grandly it rose to the occasion we
all know. In every presiding elder the League soon
found a friend, and in every district it found orators
ready to champion its cause, so that when at last, grown
to enormous proportions, it must have a general secretary of its own, it was wisely said his most important
work would after all be, not so much that of the platform as that of the office, in the preparation of literature and the administration of the organization.

The future career and the character of the Epworth

League were really foreshadowed in that famous Cleveland meeting. There the devotional spirit was dominant. To our mind, as we now recall those scenes, nothing could be more impressive than the frequent pauses in the deliberations that time might be given to prayer. Turning from the perplexing problems under discussion, again and again those earnest seekers for truth and light fell upon their knees and appealed to the great Head of the Church for wisdom and guidance in the shaping of issues which all felt must prove momentous.

In that little frame building—that little church edifice destined to a singular renown—the Epworth League was born amid those same spiritual influences that have marked its triumphal way. In its aspiration for consecrated culture, in its evangelistic spirit, in its looking up in order to lift up, its combination of aspiration and service, this youthful organization bears unmistakable marks of its alleged maternity. A true daughter of Methodism, the Epworth League has a right to the family name.

III. BY REV. CHARLES A. LITTLEFIELD, OF THE YOUNG PEOPLE'S CHRISTIAN LEAGUE.

THE men of the Cleveland conference impressed me. They were a guarantee against ill-advised action. Young, old; progressive, conservative; theoretical, practical. All were spiritual; some intensely, some conservatively, but all sincerely. There were business men of sagacity, generosity, and demonstrated worth to the Church. There were "evangelists, pastors, and teachers." Their gifts were as diversified as their callings. There were keenness of insight, practical prudence, knowledge of men and of measures; those who could plan, those who could execute; those who could see the needs of the hour, those who could quickly reduce them to propositions. There were conscientiousness, industry, seriousness, joviality, philosophy, and wit. There were unmistakably those who had the "gift of tongues," but all had the supreme gift of love, manifested in this— being strongly tested it never failed. The spirit of the memorable conference was manifestly prophetic. I think no member present—whether his own peculiar views were accepted or not, whether the final organization exactly suited him or not—escaped the impression, at the time, that that conference had given birth to a great movement.

One of the most important questions to be decided by the conference was that of name. To delineate, to designate, to suggest, to invite—these were necessary functions of a well-chosen name. "Epworth" is happy in all these functions. But this fortunate name was not chosen without much deliberation and difficulty. The writer was a member of the committee on "names," and ventures to give some of the facts not clearly brought out in the published records. The best report that the committee were able to make was that we had agreed as to the name "League," but could not agree on an adjective. A majority, however, favored "Wesley League." This the writer urgently opposed, believing that a better name could be chosen, though as yet no name had been suggested to which he would have given his support on a final vote. On receiving this report the conference went into a committee of the whole for the

consideration of a name. During the discussion which
followed, in some remarks by Robert R. Doherty,
in an attempt to say "Oxford League and Epworth
Hymnal," by a slip of the tongue he said "Oxford
Hymnal and Epworth League." This funny exchange
of adjectives raised a laugh, and apparently no more was
thought of it except that the brother sitting by my side
(Rev. J. S. Reager) and I exchanged a word of comment
upon it in which it was remarked that "Epworth
League" would not be a bad name. From that moment
"Epworth League" satisfied my hitherto unsatisfied
intuitions as to a name. From that moment I felt confident that the final outcome would be that "Epworth
League" would be chosen to designate the name of our
organization. At that point adjournment was taken for
dinner. On the way to dinner I called the attention of
my colleagues, Brothers Haven and Odell, to "Epworth
League" as a name, and declared to them my purpose
immediately on the opening of the afternoon session to
gain the floor and earnestly advocate its adoption. This
I did in a speech of about five minutes. Ten other
speeches followed, in which "Epworth" received some
support but much opposition. An informal vote was
then taken, and, to the surprise of many, while "Wesley
League" received a plurality, having twelve votes,
"Epworth" came next, with nine. It was then voted
that the name "Wesley League" be recommended, and.
the committee of the whole rose. After an earnest discussion the recommendation was adopted, and "Wesley
League" was chosen as the name of the proposed
society. The question of a name was then supposed to
be settled, but a strange intuition still clung to me that

"Epworth" was yet to be the name. As the afternoon wore away, and the evening came, and troubled seas were about us, hardly any word was uttered, but there was an apparent undercurrent of growing dissatisfaction with the name which had been selected. And yet it seemed to be taken for granted that it must stand. But when, in the evening session, the clouds hung heaviest it occurred to me to formulate the prevailing sentiment, as to certain differences, into a series of propositions, upon the basis of which an organization could be perfected. The first of these five propositions boldly declared, in the face of the name already selected, that the name of our organization should be the "Epworth League." Immediately upon the presentation of these propositions it was apparent that they met with favor, and especially the one in reference to a name. A recess of five minutes was taken for informal talk, at the expiration of which the propositions were unanimously adopted "in toto," and *Epworth League* was our name. From this point the work of organization was easy, rapid, and soon completed.

At the outset of the conference it was agreed that a representative of each of the five societies should present its scheme for a basis of union. The societies were called upon in order of their organization. Henry Date reported for the Alliance : (1) Uniform Constitution ; (2) Autonomy; (3) A strong spiritual element. Robert R. Doherty, for the Oxford League, reported that the "representatives of the League were unable as yet to make suggestions for the proposed union." W. I. Haven, President of the Christian League, reported for us of New England. The subject-matter of his report

·had been carefully talked over and agreed upon by
Brothers Haven, Odell, and myself on our way to Cleveland. But not one principle was held by us other than ·
to be conceded if necessary to organization. The
recommendations were: "(1) Publishing interests
centered in New York; (2) General organization
centered in New York; (3) General secretary to be the
Corresponding Secretary of the Sunday School Union;
(4) General Conference district organizations—to a large
degree autonomous—these to elect two delegates to a
convention to be held quadrennially at the seat of the
General Conference; (5) Local Constitution with and
without Pledge; (6) Board of Control, composed of delegates from General Conference districts, of bishops and
others." This was a more detailed outline than any
other delegation presented, and contained substantially
all that others subsequently suggested, except as to
minor details. These propositions were not *contended
for* by us.

I do not think that it particularly occurred to any
one of our delegation whether or not we were get-
ting what we had suggested. The final result, however, showed that the organization of the "Epworth
League," when all were in agreement, and all seemed
measurably satisfied, was substantially an indorsement
and incorporation of these principles. I speak of this
simply to show that in point of fact at the outset we
were all there to seek union upon the same principles.
What did not appear at first became clearly manifest in
the end, and the organization of the "Epworth League"
was quickly, harmoniously, and, we believe, providen-
tially effected.

IV. BY REV. SAMUEL PLANTZ, PH.D., OF THE METHODIST
YOUNG PEOPLE'S UNION.

IT was a quiet gathering, that Cleveland conference.
It came together unheralded, and departed almost un-
noticed. Even the church press was disposed to ignore
it. After it was over a bishop said in our hearing that
it was "the weakest and silliest thing ever done in
Methodism." Many felt it had overstepped its authority. But there was destiny in it.

As we look back upon the conference we are impressed with the excellence of its *personnel*. All present had given long and thoughtful study to the
question of young people's societies, and had been per-
sonally identified with previous movements, having in
several cases proposed their plan of organization.
While the majority were young and full of enthusiasm,
there was a sufficient number of men of maturer years to
give the meeting ballast. The clergy predominated, but
the laity had strong representatives of the opinions of
the whole Church. All proved themselves men of fine
Christian spirit and no small degree of self-control.
Two showed that they were possessed of rare diplomatic
skill and knew just when to pour oil upon the troubled
waters. Once when the convention had broken up, and
fire was beginning to show in some eyes, the day was
saved by one of these brethren moving that we pray.
An hour of knee work smoothed antagonisms, and out
of it came the Epworth League. And here is the
pleasantest memory we have of the conference, namely,
that when one of the delegations withdrew those who
remained did not rashly unite without them, but pro-

ceeded to ask the Lord to unravel the tangle into
which things had become involved.

Another thing which impresses us in retrospect is
that the conference knew at the moment it was called
to order just what it wanted to do. Its work was not
hazy, undefined, and in the mists. All had been intelli-
gently thought out, the attitude of the delegations had
evidently been agreed upon, and the disposition was
present to grapple with the difficulties in a spirit of fairness to all concerned. A union everyone was determined to have. While one delegation seemed to some to
wish to have this union effected on the basis with which
the cat unites with the mouse, still, unless nearly all
had been ready to sacrifice almost everything for which
they had previously contended, they could not possibly
have come together. We are sure, also, that every member present fully realized the importance of what was
being done. He felt that the good of Methodism demanded the consolidation of its young people's organizations. Otherwise money would be uselessly expended,
strife engendered, and the unity of the Church affected.
Moreover, he knew that at no other time could the union
be so easily accomplished, as the societies were rapidly
growing and becoming more intrenched. He knew,
also, the criticisms that would follow the conference.
This made the sessions intense in interest and sense of
responsibility. We have been asked if the Cleveland
conference had any idea of the greatness of the movement it was inaugurating. We think it did, and do not
believe that the growth of the Epworth League has
been any greater than most present expected it to be.

Again, in reviewing those days of earnest work we are

likewise impressed with the fact that nearly all those things for which the majority contended, but which were finally surrendered to consummate the union, have since become accomplished facts. Some of these things were : What should constitute the Board of Control ? Should the League have an organ separate from *Our Youth ?* Should a secretary be elected separate from the Secretary of the Sunday School Union ? Should headquarters be established in the West ? Should not the finances of the League be secured from the profits of its publications ? If the voice of the majority had ruled in the Cleveland conference we should have had at the start the Epworth League almost as it is to-day ; and one of the things that surprises us in looking backward is that in so brief a conference so great an organization could have been planned so well. We also think that the slower process by which some of these things have been secured has been for the best.

In conclusion let me say that as one of the participants in the Cleveland conference I am rejoiced to see that our young people are so fully realizing its ideals. They are keeping it as it was intended to be, an emphatically religious organization, and at the same time are finding in it a source of pure social life and intellectual culture. I feel confident that in centuries to come Methodism will find the League a strong right arm of power.

V. BY REV. J. S. REAGER, OF THE NORTH OHIO CONFER-
ENCE METHODIST EPISCOPAL ALLIANCE.

ON the morning of May 14, 1889, there assembled in Central Methodist Episcopal Church, Cleveland, O., representatives from the various young people's so-
5

cieties throughout our great denomination. They met
for a purpose ; they were moved by an all-conquering
love. All saw the need of a great spiritual and spiritu-
alizing organization for young Methodists. They talked
together as brothers and prayed with and for each
other as those who loved the Lord Jesus.

There comes over me as I write the impressions of
that first hour of devotion before we entered upon the
important business that was to occupy our undivided
attention till far into the night of the 15th. Mingled
with our devotion was a kind of gladiatorial spirit that
could be read in the faces and felt in the bearing of
men who felt the burden of personal responsibility as
representatives of organizations that had already
achieved large success and gave promise for increased
usefulness in the future.

There were Doherty and Hurlbut, with their coad-
jutors, Freeman, Docking, and Price, champions of
Oxford, with its high scholastic ideas and its purpose
for an all-round culture, and with them stood Helman
with his perfected machinery by which the " Oxford
idea " was projected with new and conquering impulse
upon the Church. I recall with admiration the fidelity
of these able champions. Then there were Cooper,
Carrel, Cogshall, Date, Heald, and Keen, in royal armor
as the advocates of the Young People's Methodist Alliance, which stood for the highest measure of spiritual
experience and the most knightly loyalty to church
discipline. Then there was the unconquerable but
sweetly submissive trio of the Young People's Christian
League—Haven, Odell, and Littlefield. Earnestly they
represented and advocated their society, and as grace-

fully consented that all should be absorbed to appear in the grander union which their faith saw as the outcome of this conference. "The Methodist Young People's Union" was borne upon the banners of six men who would be knightly champions of any noble cause— Washburn, Jacklin, Spencer, Smart, Plantz, and Morgan. Easily all hearts warmed toward these brethren who were there in the broad interests of a common Methodism and wanted the grace and wisdom of the conference to crystallize in a union cultured and spiritual enough to embrace universal Methodism. The North Ohio Conference Methodist Episcopal Alliance was born for consolidation. Whatever might be the consummated union, the object of its existence would be accomplished. The representatives of this society were evenly divided in favor of an enlarged Oxford League and of a readjusted society in which all old forms and names should be absorbed. Hoadley, Mills, and Warner were strongly wedded to Oxford; Reeder, Badgley, and the writer had nothing to contend for but the union of all Methodism under one name and banner.

It is pleasant after four years of test and triumph to recall the scenes of those memorable days. We seemed at times to be at polar distances from each other, but a song and prayer would eliminate space and bring us heart to heart again. There were two things noticeable throughout the deliberations, and by which I was deeply impressed. First, the intense earnestness of every delegate. There appeared to be conviction upon every heart that the final action was to be of far-reaching and vital importance to Methodism. Second, the fairness of statement and the charity in discussion. There

seemed to be no hidden purpose in the heart of any
delegate. All was frankness, though there were widely
divergent views as to methods. There was absolute
freedom from acrimony ; all debate was in the sweetest
charity. When the friends of the Oxford League, feeling that they had gone as far in concessions as their
honest convictions would permit, withdrew from the
deliberations, there was not a word of censure or bitter-
ness from either side. Those who remained went at
once into a committee of the whole to besiege the
throne of grace for guidance. I can never forget that
prayer meeting. As I look at the wonderful results
of these four years of Epworth League history I am
constrained to believe that in the heart throes of that
hour God bowed the heavens and came down to set his
seal upon the brotherly fidelity of his servants. When
after a brief counsel all came together once more a consummation was immediately reached. Who of all that
company can doubt that it was God's immediate answer
to prayer ?

The incident of the name was peculiar, and I think
providential. This was a hotly contested point. Oxford's friends held stoutly for a continuance of this
honor, while many of us felt that a new name would
bear with it more enthusiasm. One name after another
had been suggested, but no agreement had been reached.
Noon adjournment was upon us, and a vote was about
to be taken on several names. Dr. Doherty, as an advocate for Oxford, in closing a brief speech, by a *lapsus
linguæ* spoke of the "Oxford Hymnal," which by con-
trast suggested to me Epworth League. This I at once
proposed as the name most appropriate because nearest

the life of our great founder; later on this name was adopted with practical unanimity.

My faith now is that the entire result was of divine direction. If our Epworth League holds to its aims, "the highest New Testament standard of Christian experience," and a roundly cultivated manhood and womanhood, and continues to look up and lift up, most glorious results will follow for Christ and the Church. The members of this conference will by and by hold a jubilee in heaven, and with a united Methodism on earth and in glory give honor and praise to our blessed Lord for the spirit of wisdom and brotherliness by which the League was formed to bless the world.

CHAPTER V.

THE FIRST MEETING OF THE BOARD OF CONTROL.

THE Board of Control met for the first time at Chicago on February 6, 1890. The meeting attracted wide attention. Many eager spectators were present at the various sessions. Some new faces appeared. Several familiar ones were missing. Dr. Jesse L. Hurlbut called the meeting to order, and Dr. W. H. W. Rees, of Iowa, was chosen scribe. Then followed a season of devotion. The appointment of committees came next. Later the Committee on Permanent Organization reported the name of Bishop James N. FitzGerald for president and that of Dr. W. H. W. Rees for secretary. The Committee on Credentials recognized the following members of the Board:

Appointed by the bishops: Bishop J. N. FitzGerald, Rev. W. H. W. Rees, D.D., Rev. M. D. Carrel, Rev. A. H. Gillet, D.D., Rev. W. I. Haven. Appointed by the Sunday School Union: Rev. J. L. Hurlbut, D.D., Robert R. Doherty, Ph.D., B. E. Helman, Rev. F. Mason North, Rev. Crandall J. North. Appointed by the Tract Society: Rev. J. M. Freeman, D.D., Rev. J. T. Docking, John Bentley, Rev. E. S. Osbon, D.D., Rev. J. E. Price, D.D. Elected from the General Conference districts: First District—William Flanders, Rev. J. W. Dearborn; Second District—Rev. J. H. Coleman, D.D., Richard Lavery; Third and Fourth Districts unrepresented; Fifth District—O. L. Doty, C. H. Moore; Sixth District—Rev. Vaughan S. Collins, Rev. L. E. Prentiss, D.D.; Seventh District—Rev. H. J. Talbott, D.D.; Eighth District—Rev. Arthur Edwards, D.D., W. W. Cooper; Ninth District—Rev. T. McK. Stuart, D.D., Rev. H. C. Jennings; Tenth District—B. L. Paine, M.D., Rev. D. C. Winship; Eleventh District unrepresented; Twelfth District—Rev. J. B. Young, D.D., Rev. Frank Lenig; Thirteenth District unrepresented ; Fourteenth District—Rev. G. L. Cole, Rollo V. Watt.

On recommendation of the committee Rev. Henry Liebhart, D.D., of the Thirteenth District, Rev. I. B. Scott, D.D., of the Eleventh District, and Rev. C. E. Bacon were permitted to engage in the deliberations of the body. Reports were made by the corresponding secretary, which showed clearly that the work of organization had been progressing rapidly, and that the League was meeting with a cordial reception in all sections of the Church. Committees were constituted as follows : 1. Committee on Constitution of the Board of Control—J. E. Price, J. L. Hurlbut, L. E. Prentiss, M. D. Carrel, J. T. Docking, H. C. Jennings, C. J. North, G. L. Cole. 2. Committee on Local Chapter Constitution—W. I. Haven, Robert R. Doherty, W. W. Cooper, A. H. Gillet, O. L. Doty. 3. Committee on Finance— B. L. Paine, T. McK. Stuart, Richard Lavery, R. V. Watt, John Bentley. 4. Committee on Literature—Arthur Edwards, W. H. W. Rees, E. S. Osbon, V. S. Collins, C. H. Moore, J. B. Young. 5. Committee on Relation to Other Young People's Societies—J. W. Dearborn, H. J. Talbott, W. M. Flanders, J. L. Hurlbut.

The Committee on Constitution presented its report,

and after much discussion and no little modification it was adopted. The Constitution read as follows :

ARTICLE I. *Name.*—This organization shall be known as the Epworth League of the Methodist Episcopal Church.

ARTICLE II. *Object.*—The object of this organization is to promote an earnest, intelligent, practical, and loyal piety in the young members and friends of the Church ; to aid them in constant growth in grace and in the attainment of purity of heart.

ARTICLE III. *Membership.*—Any young people's society in the Methodist Episcopal Church may become a chapter of the Epworth League, provided that it adopts the aims and general plans of the League, that its president and officers and methods of works are approved by the pastor and official board or Quarterly Conference, on being enrolled at the central office.

ARTICLE IV. *Government.*—The Epworth League shall be governed by a Board of Control to be chosen as follows : Five members to be appointed by the Board of Bishops ; five members to be appointed by the Board of Managers of the Sunday School Union, of whom the Corresponding Secretary of the Union shall be one ; five members by the Board of Managers of the Tract Society ; and two members from each General Conference district, these members to be chosen as the organization in each General Conference district may desire. All the members of this board shall continue in office for the term of two years or until their successors are elected. The Board of Control shall meet annually at such time and place as it shall designate at its previous session.

ARTICLE V. *Officers.*—The officers of the General League shall be a corresponding secretary, a recording secretary, and a treasurer. There shall also be an Executive Committee of seven, three of whom shall be the officers named. At least four of the seven shall be chosen from the representatives of the Board of Control from the General Conference districts, all these officers and members of the Executive Committee to be elected by ballot by the Board of Control at each annual meeting.

ARTICLE VI. *Amendments.*—This Constitution may be amended at any annual meeting of the Board of Control by a two-thirds vote of those present and voting, notice having been given three months previously to the Executive Committee and published in the organ of the Epworth League.

The next report of especial interest was that on literature. It read as follows :

The Epworth League, which has two thousand chapters and over one hundred thousand members, thinks it ought to have an organ. Though the friends of our various church papers may suggest that these papers can meet the wants of the churches as to Epworth news and discussion, the League's thorough persuasion that a special organ is needed is beyond controversy, and there is nothing of wisdom left but to proceed to supply that inevitable want. The expression of the desire is general that this General Board of Control should proceed to supply the need. The present organ is *Our Youth*, printed in New York. It is only frank and accurate to say that this paper in its present form and proportions and plans is an inadequate mouthpiece for a League of these proportions. If it is proposed to modify *Our Youth* we must begin by changing its name and elevating the muzzles of its guns so that it may reach young people older by several years than are that paper's present readers. Our organ should contain more space, and its general make-up should be utterly changed.

We suggest that the new paper should cost less. Its maximum price for a single copy should not be more than $1, and when taken in clubs sent to one address each increase of ten subscribers should reduce the price one dime, thus : One copy should be $1; ten copies should be 90 cents ; twenty copies should be 80 cents ; thirty copies should be 70 cents ; forty copies should be 60 cents ; fifty copies should be 50 cents. At this point the reduction should stop, lest some eager agent should procure a club of one hundred and claim that at that rate the paper should be sent gratis.

This committee is persuaded that the paper ordained as the organ of the League should be chiefly given over to League affairs. There ought not to be a minimum space allowed to our work, but there should, on the contrary, be included full news from fellow League workers, and abundant space for articles and quotations from allied literature, so that readers may feel that they are placed in contact

each week with the consecrated brain and heart of all who are labor-
ing on parallel lines in sister Churches.

We heartily hope that our organ may be issued by the Book Concern, which is able to pay the bills during the youth of the enterprise,
and which is already in communication with the Church's ministerial
agents in the East, West, North, and South.   While the paper is
struggling to its "paying basis" it can be fostered by those who have
learned the secret of compelling publishing success.   As a corollary,
we are willing that when the organ of this League reaches a paying
point the profits shall go into the superannuate fund for the support
of worn-out preachers and their dependent families.   We shall hail
the day when this League·is glorified by sharing in the support of
our disabled fathers in the ministry.   In that one respect we antedate
the day when our young people may be exalted by association with
older members of our Church in caring for our beloved pulpit pioneers.

With this understanding we suggest that a memorial be sent to our
Publishing Committee, which meets in New York next week.   We
recommend that that body be requested to authorize our book agents
to supply us an organ after the pattern sketched in this report.   It is
our hope that the paper finally fixed upon shall be based on the paper
known as *Our Youth*, after its name has been changed and its scope
widened, or that an utterly new paper be authorized in order to meet
the needs and desires of our rapidly growing Epworth host.   We
particularly hope that the new organ may appear without unnecessary
delay.   This is the precious planting-time of Epworth seed.   We are
unwilling to make needless experiments or to take on further trial
appliances which are already proven inadequate.   If we can have a
prompt, roomy, enthusiastic, and adequate organ we hereby pledge
to it our unqualified and undivided support and advocacy and gratitude.   We desire to have a connectional and loyal Methodist League
and organ of the League.   We hope for two thousand more chapters,
and more than one hundred thousand more members, in the near
future.   By hard work and unflagging zeal we hope to give the new
paper fifty thousand subscribers before the next General Conference
session.   Until the paper is established we cannot prescribe as to its
editorship.   As to that point we are willing to leave the editorial
administration in the hands of the Book Committee, knowing that
our voice in the future will be regarded fraternally and effectually.

A committee, consisting of Revs. Arthur Edwards, T. McK. Stuart, J. E. Price, C. J. North, and W. I. Haven, was requested to present the memorial of the Literature Committee to the Book Committee.

The election of officers resulted in the choice of Dr. Hurlbut as corresponding secretary, Robert R. Doherty as recording secretary, Dr. Freeman as treasurer; and these three, together with W. W. Cooper, Dr. Prentiss, O. L. Doty, and Dr. Edwards, were constituted an Executive Committee.

The candid utterance of the Board of Control on the relation of the Epworth League to other young people's societies was significant, especially in the light of later developments. The report of the committee adopted by the Board read :

The Epworth League had its origin in the conviction that the various young people's societies of the Church should be united in one organization. Its scheme of work has been made large enough to comprehend all forms of Christian activity. We therefore recommend that all literary, social, and religious societies of young people now in existence in our Church merge themselves into the Epworth League, and that every such society continue its special work through that department of the League under which it would properly fall.

We cordially recognize the efficient work of the societies of Christian Endeavor and other similar organizations. We disclaim any purpose of antagonism. We seek rather that efficiency that comes in the use of our own Church methods. We would join hands with them all in the training and leadership of young minds in aggressive work for our one Master. To this end we recommend that our Leagues seek such cooperation with all other Christian societies of young people in systematic visitation of the unchurched and poor, in temperance and other reforms which may require division of labor or united effort.

We recommend the appointment of a fraternal delegate to the Epworth League of the Methodist Church of Canada.

We recommend the appointment of a committee of five which shall
seek the appointment of committees from similar societies who shall
arrange for an interdenominational conference of young people's
societies.

In obedience to the recommendations of this commit-
tee W. W. Cooper was chosen fraternal delegate to the
Epworth League of Canada, and Dr. J. B. Young to the
Young People's Society of Christian Endeavor. Drs.
Hurlbut and Young were appointed a committee on an
international conference.

The report of the Committee on Local Constitution
precipitated a spirited discussion, but after the smoke
of battle had cleared away it was found that the original
plan of the committee was not seriously modified. The
local Constitution as finally adopted read as follows:

ARTICLE I. *Name.*—This organization shall be known as the
Epworth League of the ——, Methodist Episcopal Church of ——,
and shall be subordinate to the Quarterly Conference of said Church,
and a chapter of the Epworth League of the Methodist Episcopal
Church.

ARTICLE II. *Object.*—The object of the League is to promote intelligent and loyal piety in the young members and friends of the
Church ; to aid them in the attainment of purity of heart and in constant growth in grace, and to train them in works of mercy and help.

ARTICLE III. *Membership.*—1. Members shall be constituted by
election of the chapter, on nomination of the president, after approval by the cabinet. 2. The pastor shall be *ex officio* a member
of the chapter and the cabinet. 3. Wherever a chapter decides,
there shall be two classes of members, active and associate. Active
members shall, in addition to election as provided in Section 1, subscribe to the following pledge :

I will earnestly seek for myself, and do what I can to help others attain, the
highest New Testament standard of experience and life. I will abstain from all
those forms of worldly amusement forbidden by the Discipline of the Methodist
Episcopal Church, and I will attend, so far as possible, the religious meetings of
the chapter and the church, and take some active part in them.

Active members only shall be eligible to election as officers of the chapter. Associate members shall be entitled to all other privileges of membership.

ARTICLE IV. *Departments.*—The work of the League shall be carried on through six departments, as follows: 1. Department of Christian Work. 2. Department of Mercy and Help. 3. Department of Literary Work. 4. Department of Entertainment. 5. Department of Correspondence. 6. Department of Finance. The distribution of work under each department shall be as follows: 1. Department of Christian Work : (*a*) Young people's prayer meeting; (*b*) spiritual welfare of members ; (*c*) Christian work among the young ; (*d*) Sunday-school interests ; (*e*) missionary work ; (*f*) open-air meetings. 2. Department of Mercy and Help: (*a*) Systematic visitation ; (*b*) temperance ; (*c*) tract distribution ; (*d*) Junior League work ; (*e*) home mission work ; (*f*) social purity ; (*g*) employment bureau. 3. Department of Literary Work : (*a*) Bible study ; (*b*) lectures and literary work ; (*c*) lyceums, libraries, and educational work ; (*d*) church literature; (*e*) Epworth League readings; (*f*) C. L. S. C. readings. 4. Department of Entertainment : (*a*) Reception and introduction of members ; (*b*) socials and social entertainments ; (*c*) music for all meetings : (*d*) excursions and picnics ; (*e*) amusements for all meetings ; (*f*) badges and signals. 5. Department of Correspondence : (*a*) All records ; (*b*) correspondence with central office ; (*c*) correspondence with absent members ; (*d*) historical and other statistics ; (*e*) record of literary work. 6. Department of Finance : (*a*) All regular finance ; (*b*) expenses of all departments ; (*c*) collection of dues ; (*d*) raising funds ; (*e*) expenditures.

ARTICLE V. *Officers.*—1. The officers shall be a president, secretary, treasurer, first vice president, second vice president, third vice president, and fourth vice president. 2. The president, who shall be a member of the Methodist Episcopal Church, shall be elected by ballot on a majority vote. The other officers shall be members of the Methodist Episcopal or some other evangelical Church, and shall be elected in the same manner. 3. All officers must be approved by the Quarterly Conference or the official board. 4. After approval by the Quarterly Conference or official board the names of the officers, with their addresses, shall be promptly forwarded to the central office of the Epworth League. 5. The officers shall perform the duties usually assigned to such officers. They shall also, in the order named, represent and have charge of the Departments of Correspondence, Finance, Christian Work, Mercy and Help, Literary Work, and Entertainment. They shall, together with the president, constitute the cabinet of the chapter, aiding the president as he may request. 6. For the purpose of enlisting all in the work and rendering it more effective, the cabinet shall assign each member to at least one department of work. Each cabinet officer shall name to the chapter a committee of from three to five members for the management of his department, the officer being *ex officio* chairman.

ARTICLE VI. *Meetings.*—The chapter shall hold a devotional meeting on ——— evening of each week, to be led by one of the members of the chapter under the direction of the Committee on Christian Work. Other meetings shall be held as the cabinet may arrange for them.

ARTICLE VII. *By-laws and Amendments.*—The chapter may adopt such by-laws consistent with the Constitution as may be needed. Amendments to Constitution or By-laws must be submitted in writing to the cabinet, and when approved by it may be adopted by a two-thirds vote of those present at any regular meeting.

The meeting lasted two days. On the evening of the second day a mass meeting was held in the auditorium of First Church. Bishop FitzGerald presided and delivered a thoughtful, vigorous address. Dr. J. L. Hurlbut, Dr. W. H. W. Rees, Rev. W. I. Haven, and Rev. M. D. Carrel also spoke briefly. The Board adjourned to meet in St. Louis, on May 14, 1891.

CHAPTER VI.

STARTING "THE EPWORTH HERALD."

REFERENCE has been made in the previous chapter to the action of the Board of Control upon the question of an official League paper. No sketch of the beginnings of the League movement would be complete without some reference to the launching of our organ.

Our Youth had for several years been the young people's paper of the Methodist Episcopal Church. Dr. John H. Vincent was its first editor, and after his election to the episcopacy Dr. Jesse L. Hurlbut succeeded to the tripod. It was a handsome, illustrated weekly of sixteen pages, and was edited with recognized ability. During its later years the paper devoted a good deal of space to the Oxford League, and when the Epworth League was formed it immediately gave the new organization proper prominence and support. Its homilies on the topics for the devotional meeting were exceptionally good. Much interesting news was gathered from the new chapters then rapidly springing up. Admirable suggestions for departmental work were also furnished from week to week. But a conviction that a paper of somewhat larger size, whose pages should be wholly devoted to the interests of the League, became general. It was emphasized by conventions in ringing resolutions. The sentiment was voiced by the Church press. Correspondents described at length and with great minute-

ness of detail just what kind of an organ the League
should have. The correspondents did not agree in
their ideals, but the publication of their views gave material aid to the projectors of the new enterprise.

The Book Committee met at New York on the second Wednesday of February, 1890. The special committee representing the Board of Control appeared before the body, and made known the wishes of the Board
concerning a paper. The committee was received with
great courtesy, and the question which it presented received patient consideration. It was decided to dis-
continue the publication of *Our Youth* after the 1st of
June following, and substitute a paper to be published
at Chicago. The details connected with the launching
of the paper, its size and price, the election of an editor,
etc., were referred to the Western section of the Book
Committee and the Western publishing agents.

A call for a meeting was immediately issued, and the
Western section convened at Chicago on March 5.
The questions involved were thoroughly canvassed. Dr.
W. P. Stowe, then publishing agent at Chicago, had prepared a "dummy" showing a paper of sixteen pages
somewhat larger than those of *Our Youth*, and a weekly
of this size and style was soon decided upon. But what
should the infant be named? That question was not
so easily answered. Various cognomens were suggested.
Some one proposed *The Epworth News*. Another
thought that *The Epworth Standard* would be a name
around which the young people would be likely to rally.
Still another thought it would be well to give to the
new paper an orthodox Methodist name by calling it
The Epworth Advocate. But Dr. Stowe had the words

The Epworth Herald printed in plain black letters across the front page of his "dummy," and the adoption of this name he earnestly advocated. His logic, or en-thusiasm, or both, proved effective, and the publishers were authorized to fling the name *The Epworth Herald* to the breeze.

The price at which the new paper should be published occasioned a spirited discussion. The Board of Con-trol had asked for a paper at $1 per year, with graded reductions for clubs of different dimensions. But it was thought that such a paper as had been decided upon could not be profitably published at that figure. So the rate was fixed at $1.50 for single subscriptions; $1 when sent in clubs of ten; and 80 cents when supplied in quantities of twenty-five or more. As the reader al-ready knows, the price to single subscribers was reduced to $1 at the close of the first year. At this rate it is perhaps the cheapest paper of its grade in the world.

The selection of an editor next received attention. The result of the ballot was the unanimous election of the young man who pushes this pencil. Rev. Stephen J. Herben, of Jersey City, N. J., a graduate of North-western University, and a practical printer and ex-perienced newspaper correspondent, was subsequently chosen as assistant editor. The editor arrived at Chicago on April 1. An office was fitted up on the fifth floor of the Book Concern building, and preparations for issu-ing the new paper immediately began. The date of the first issue was to be June 1, but it was decided to publish an advance copy for general distribution. This "sample" appeared on May 1, though it was dated a month later. An edition of 150,000 copies was printed

6

and scattered broadcast. We insert herewith a fac-simile of the first page of the first issue. Inasmuch as it will be difficult for many to read the fine type we repro-duce, as a sort of curio, two short editorials:

SALUTATION.

The editor hereby makes his bow.
We will not write a conventional salutatory. Such effusions are apt to abound in glittering generalities, and are fruitful in promises that are rarely fulfilled. Study our name. Does not that indicate with sufficient clearness our character and mission?

The Epworth Herald is started in response to an earnest, reason-able, and widespread demand. The great and to-be-greater Epworth League felt the need of an organ thoroughly devoted to the promotion of its interests. To supply that need we shall give the best we have of heart and brain. We cannot do more than that. And we would be unworthy our place upon this important tripod should we aim to do less. Two things, however, we wish to say frankly, namely: 1. There are several things about editing a newspaper which we do not know. 2. We have no expectation of pleasing everybody. Sugges-tions from our friends will always be in order. We do not promise to adopt all the advice given us, but will invariably give it conscien-tious consideration.

We ask the loyal, enthusiastic cooperation of young Methodists and their older friends. It is *your* paper, not ours. The *Herald* must win. The publishers have planned magnificently. The field is wide. The opportunity is golden. Let every one promptly and earnestly "lend a hand." Help us to make a wide-awake, progressive, spiritual, inspiring paper—a journal worthy to be the special organ of the splendid army of young American Methodists now marshaling under the banners of the Epworth League.

NOT AN IDEAL NUMBER.

This initial issue is not an ideal one. Things are new. The big editorial chair seems strange and uncomfortable. Our scissors are stiff and unwieldy. The pastepot looks stilted and aristocratic when compared with the familiar old one we left behind. And this

The Epworth Herald.

"I desire a league, offensive and defensive, with every soldier of Jesus Christ."—*John Wesley*

CHICAGO, SATURDAY, JUNE 7, 1890.

The Epworth Herald.

OFFICIAL ORGAN OF THE EPWORTH LEAGUE

CRANSTON & STOWE
57 Washington Street, Chicago

TERMS OF SUBSCRIPTION:

The Editor's Portfolio.

SALUTATION

NOT AN IDEAL NUMBER

OUR FIELD

THE EPWORTH MOVEMENT.

WHAT IS IT?

FACSIMILE OF FIRST PAGE OF FIRST ISSUE OF " THE EP-
WORTH HERALD."

pencil is pushed by a hand that persists in trembling a bit. Nothing exactly fits. The very stars in their courses fight against the first number of a periodical. This may be taken as a *suggestion* of what future issues will be. That is all.

Our departments have been arranged after a careful study of the probable needs of our wide constituency. But they are elastic. We shall add, and subtract, and multiply, and divide as occasion seems to demand. The *Herald* is something of a pioneer in this field of journalism. The experimental period must be passed through. Special features will be added from time to time and old ones dropped. Certain issues will be given up almost exclusively to particular vital phases of League work. Symposiums, interviews, personal sketches, and so forth will be mixed in to give spice and variety. There is no stereotyping machine in this sanctum.

Unlike the fabled goddess, *The Epworth Herald* has not sprung into being "full-orbed and glorious." In harmony with the vigorous young organization of which it is the organ the paper is to grow. We have placed our ideal high up, and are going on "unto perfection."

Our new paper met with a most cordial reception. The church editors published words of welcome. Correspondents wrote their congratulations. Subscriptions began to pour in. The first list came from the Tabernacle Church of Detroit, Mich., Dr. William Dawe pastor; the second was sent by our church at Athens, Tenn. Within a month the clerks who had been assigned to duty in the business department were working extra hours to keep up with the demands of the situation.

The subsequent history of the *Herald* is so fresh in the minds of its friends that it need not be told in detail. At the close of its first year the little paper had a subscription list, after counting its inheritance of 12,000 from *Our Youth*, of 42,000. At the end of its second year the 60,000 mark had been passed. The third year closes with a list of more than 75,000. The fourth year of its history will undoubtedly give the paper a list of at least 100,000. It already has the largest circulation of any denominational weekly in the world, and is upon a very profitable financial foundation. No periodical ever had a multitude of friends who were more indulgent and loyal, and none ever passed its initial stage with more marked success.

CHAPTER VII.

THE SECOND AND THIRD MEETINGS OF THE BOARD OF CONTROL.

THE famed hospitality of the Methodists of St. Louis, together with a desire to meet the energetic Epworth workers of that region, were two things which were influential in deciding the Board of Control to hold its next session in that mid-continent city. The meeting convened on May 21, 1891, in the lecture room of Union Church. More than a year had now elapsed since the last board gathering, and the League had meanwhile developed with marvelous rapidity. Chapters had been organized at the rate of between fifty and one hundred per week, and the cause had grown in favor in all sections of the Church. It was with peculiar satisfaction, therefore, that the representatives of this wonderful young organization greeted each other on that balmy May morning, exchanged mutual congratulations, and joined in heartfelt praise to God.

Bishop FitzGerald, our beloved president, occupied the chair. Rev. M. D. Carrel led the opening devotions. For an hour the brethren sang songs of praise and besought the presence and blessing of the Lord during the important meeting which was about to open. In addition to the members of the Board a large company of interested visitors was present. Among these were Bishops Bowman and Hurst. These chief pastors,

together with Drs. Stowe and Fry, were invited to
participate freely in the deliberations of the Board.

Dr. J. L. Hurlbut made a report which bristled with
points of interest. Five thousand five hundred and
seventy-seven chapters were reported, a net increase
of three thousand seven hundred since the last meeting. Marked increase in the devotion and efficiency of
our members was also gladly acknowledged. "The
Epworth League," said the doctor, "is more than a mere
aggregation of numbers. It is rapidly becoming a
disciplined army of young soldiers of the cross. We
observe every day the evidences of the spiritual power
and progress of the League. Every mail brings testi-
monies to our office; we hear them in the reports of
presiding elders and pastors at the Annual Conferences;
we meet them everywhere in district conventions. . . .
I believe that this awakening will still advance; that our
young people will become clearer in their religious
experience, stronger in their testimony, more aspiring
after holiness of heart, more fully consecrated in the
Master's service, and more earnest in labors for his
cause."

Dr. J. M. Freeman, treasurer, made a financial statement which showed a small balance upon the right side
of the League ledger. Recording Secretary Doherty
read the minutes of the sessions of the Executive Committee which had been held since the last board meeting.
After a spirited debate the appointment of four general
committees was decided upon, namely, on Memorial
to the General Conference, on Literature, on Resolutions,
and on Finance. To these were subsequently added
special committees on the American University and on

Ecumenical Relations between the Epworth Leagues of the different branches of Methodism.

One of the most interesting features of the afternoon session was furnished by the reports from the General Conference districts. They were full of inspiration and encouragement. Advancement and victory was the glad story told by every speaker. The Committee on the American University recommended that great enterprise to the confidence of the young people of the Church, and the report was heartily adopted. Bishop Hurst spoke his appreciation and thanks.

A mass meeting was held at night. The auditorium was tastefully decorated with tropical plants, cut flowers, and appropriate Epworth mottoes. In the multitude were brigades of Epworthians from the local Methodist Episcopal churches and those of the Methodist Episcopal churches, South. Bishop Bowman presided, and was in his happiest mood. The first address was made by Dr. Hurlbut. It was an inspiring putting of League aims and possibilities. The editor of *The Epworth Herald* followed. Dr. Doherty delivered a clear-cut and winning address on "Consecration." Bishop FitzGerald spoke last. He was exceedingly happy and forceful in his remarks, and was enthusiastically cheered. At the close of the formal program a reception was given in the lecture room by the young people. It was a delightful affair.

On Friday morning the reports of the committees were listened to. The Committee on Local Constitution proposed several minor changes, but after full discussion they were almost all laid upon the table. The Committee on Literature submitted through Chairman Osbon a report expressing great satisfaction with the character and make-up of *The Epworth Herald*, and congratulated the League upon its phenomenal success. The committee recommended the publication of a series of leaflets illustrating the work of the different departments, to be sold at a price not to exceed five cents per copy.

Mr. J. W. Baer, General Secretary of the Young People's Society of Christian Endeavor, was introduced and made fraternal remarks. The Committee on Ecumenical Relations reported through Rev. W. I. Haven. It recommended the appointment of a standing committee on Ecumenical Relations whose duty it should be to secure as soon as possible the organization of the League in all the different branches of Methodism. The report also advised that a League rally be held in connection with the Ecumenical Conference at Washington, and that an international League gathering be held at the earliest proper hour. This report was heartily adopted. So was a report indorsing the organization of Oxford chapters in colleges and universities where Methodist students attend.

A commission was appointed to prepare a memorial to the coming General Conference, asking for the recognition of the Epworth League as a regular connectional society of the Church. This was the *personnel* of the Commission: Bishop FitzGerald, T. McKendree Stuart, R. R. Doherty, M. D. Carrel, W. I. Haven, L. E. Prentiss, and J. H. Coleman. The Commission was instructed to submit the memorial to the next meeting of the Board of Control for approval or amendment.

The vote of thanks to Rev. Dr. C. P. Masden and the friends of Union Church for the generous hospitality with which they had entertained their Epworth guests was passed with enthusiasm, and meant more than such formal expressions often do. No sooner was the board adjourned than Mr. S. C. Buckingham, Mr. C. G. Bowman, and others took the brethren in charge. They conducted them to the Mississippi River, where a fine excursion steamer was already crowded with the young Methodists of St. Louis. For several hours a delightful ride was enjoyed, the boat returning in time for the visitors to embark on the evening trains for their respective homes.

During the last few days of April, 1892, many Methodist eyes were turned toward the city of Omaha, where the delegates to the General Conference were assembling. On the opposite bank of the Missouri River stands Council Bluffs, Ia., where our Board of Control had been called to meet five days before the opening of the great quadrennial legislature. The special object of this meeting was the consideration of the report of the Commission which had been appointed a year before to draft a formal memorial to the General Conference.

The members were all present excepting four, namely, Dr. A. H. Gillet, Rev. F. Mason North, John Bentley, and W. W. Cooper. Rev. J. M. Meeker served as alternate for Mr. North, Rev. Frank Lenig for Mr. Bentley, and Rev. Frederick A. Smart for Mr. Cooper. Mr. C. E. Piper, of Chicago, was introduced as the successor of Dr. Edwards, and the doctor was invited to participate in the business of the session. Revs. D. N. McInturff

and M. F. Colburn were also present as representatives
from the Pacific coast.

Soon after the opening the Commission presented its
report. It was temporarily laid upon the table pending
the presentation of other memorials on the same subject. One came from the Fifth General Conference
District, one from the Sixth, and one from the Eighth.
The Topeka, Kan., District also presented a plan of
general organization. The debate on the memorial was
decidedly animated. Almost the entire afternoon session of Thursday and both sessions of Friday were taken
up with a consideration of the vital document. Every
sentence was discussed separately, and almost every
sentence was changed, sometimes more than once.
When Saturday morning dawned apparently very little
had been settled. Realizing that the Board must soon
adjourn, the brethren addressed themselves with great
earnestness to the business before them. By afternoon
they were ready to consider the adoption of the memorial as a whole, but before doing so, and for the purpose of securing the wisest possible form of expression,
it was decided to reconsider the entire document article
by article. Motions, amendments, and substitutes followed each other in rapid succession. It was very
amusing when the minutes were read to listen to the
record of nine consecutive motions, each of which was
laid upon the table. But as night drew on the memorial
as finally amended was adopted. This document, which
had been the occasion of so much thought, and over
which such a vast amount of eloquence had been
poured out, was then placed in the hands of a committee consisting of such members of the Board as were

also members of the General Conference, together with Arthur Edwards and J. F. Berry, with a request that it be submitted to the Conference at the earliest practicable date.

Various other items of business received attention. The General Conference was requested to arrange for the printing of League statistics in the Minutes of the Annual Conferences and in the General Minutes. A committee was appointed to secure designs for a new badge. Action was taken that enabled the local cabinet by unanimous vote and with the concurrence of the pastor, to drop the names of unworthy members for causes which it deemed sufficient.

Before final adjournment on Saturday night a most spiritual service was held. Earnest prayer was offered for the Lord's blessing upon the work of the past three days, and for benedictions upon the General Conference soon to assemble. It was a time of heart searching and consecration, and will not soon be forgotten by those who participated. There was a feeling of uncertainty in reference to just what the great body might do for the League, and after adjournment most of the brethren betook themselves to Omaha to await with some anxiety the result.

CHAPTER VIII.

THE LEAGUE IN THE GENERAL CONFERENCE.

FOR many months before the gathering of the General Conference of 1892 it was freely admitted by our most intelligent church leaders that no questions were likely to come before the body of more vital importance than those involved in the proposed official recognition of the Epworth League. The probable action of the Conference had been widely canvassed. It was well known that almost every one of the five hundred delegates entertained for the League feelings of the utmost friendliness. But these men, coming as they did from widely separated sections of the Church, were almost sure to view matters from different angles of vision, and were unlikely, therefore, to reach harmonious conclusions without some earnest debate.

The Conference convened at Omaha on the 1st of May, but three days elapsed before the great body was organized and duly "seated." On the afternoon of the 4th of May the delegates assembled at First Church to arrange for certain special committees for the session. Soon after opening Dr. S. E. Pendleton, of Kansas, arose and moved for a special committee on the Epworth League, to consist of five members at large and two from each General Conference district. This was instantly seconded in several parts of the church. A half hour was spent in determining the size of the com-

mittee, and several brief, enthusiastic speeches were made. The speakers paid a glowing tribute to our growing organization, and recounted some splendid results of its activities. These words of appreciation were received with an outburst of applause which made the special friends of the cause grateful and happy. Dr. Pendleton's motion prevailed.

On the morning of May 7 Bishop Andrews announced to the General Conference that the bishops had nominated the following special committee on the Epworth League: At large—Arthur Edwards, S. W. Heald, D. R. Lowrie, Alfred Anderson, and D. T. Denny. From the districts—1. J. M. Durrell, R. L. Douglas. 2. J. H. Coleman, Peter Welsh. 3. E. M. Mills, W. B. Wright. 4. S. W. Gehrett, T. H. Murray. 5. W. H. Rider, A. M. Mattison. 6. W. S. Edwards, James Armstrong 7. H. A. Gobin, T. J. Robinson. 8. J. F. Berry, Robert McMillan. 9. H. C. Jennings, Henry Egbert. 10. A. W. Atkinson, B. L. Paine. 11. Harry Swann, B. E. Scruggs. 12. S. E. Pendleton, H. C. De Motte. 13. Henry Liebhart, W. F. Finke. 14. E. W. Caswell, C. B. Perkins. Immediately after the committee had been named J. F. Berry presented the memorial from the Board of Control and moved the suspension of the rules so that it could properly be referred to the committee. The committee met that afternoon at the First Congregational Church for organization. Dr. D. R. Lowrie, of Newark Conference, was elected chairman, and Dr. S. E. Pendleton was chosen scribe. Dr. Lowrie found himself so occupied with other pressing duties that he could not serve, and J. F. Berry was named for the chairmanship.

Thirteen sessions of the committee were held. Those who attended them either as participants or spectators will not soon forget their experiences. No discussions which have taken place even on the floor of the General Conference could have been more animated. An alert body of men was that Epworth League committee. The members had opinions, and knew how to state them. They had convictions, and possessed courage to defend them. An honest effort had been made by the bishops in selecting the committeemen to have all possible shades of opinions regarding young people's work represented, but it soon transpired that every member was either directly identified with the League or in warm sympathy with its methods. The matter which inspired debate was not the question whether or not the League should have recognition as the young people's society of the Church, but in regard to the best possible form of permanent organization. The memorial from the Board of Control was gone over item by item. Many minor alterations were made. No serious differences of opinion were discovered, however, till the status of the young people's societies in our Church other than the Epworth League was broached. Then came a contest. It was proposed to provide for the affiliation of such societies with the League on condition that their officers and general plans of work be approved by the pastor and official board or Quarterly Conference, and that they be duly enrolled at our central office. Mr. T. H. Murray, an able lawyer from central Pennsylvania, expressed fears that the legislation we were planning would be regarded as inimical to the "other societies" then in existence in our Church, and contended with great vehemence and persistency that we should provide for them upon a more liberal basis. As a compromise it was finally agreed, with but one dissenting voice, that this clause be added to the article on organization : " But it is not hereby intended to disturb the present status of other young people's socities now organized in the Methodist Episcopal Church which are under the control of the pastor and Quarterly Conference." This, it was believed, would be a generous attitude to maintain toward those societies which had been organized before the League had an existence, and which were attached to the form of organization under which they were working. But it was assumed that new young people's organizations in our Church would invariably be Epworth Leagues.

Some discussion arose over the proposition to have a general secretary elected by the General Conference instead of by the Board of Control, but in view of the concession mentioned above those who were inclined to look with disfavor upon the plan withdrew their opposition. On Thursday morning, May 19, the chairman of the Epworth League Committee asked consent of the General Conference to present the report of that committee so that it could be printed in the *Daily Christian Advocate*. This was readily given, and the motion that the report be made the special order of the day immediately after the reading of the journal on Saturday morning was also unanimously consented to.

Saturday morning witnessed a full attendance of delegates. The galleries of the Exposition Building were also more than usually crowded with interested spectators. Many of the friends of the League were

present from different parts of the country, drawn
thither to listen to the debate and also to attend the
great mass meeting announced for the following Sabbath afternoon. The report of the committee being
called up, Dr. D. S. Monroe, secretary of the Conference, read the document in full. It was then resolved
to take up the document item by item. The discussion
consumed the entire session. With the details of the
debate the reader would not be greatly interested.
Motions, substitutes, amendments, and amendments to
amendments followed each other so rapidly that Bishop
Andrews, who was presiding, was sorely perplexed,
level-headed man though he is. Some of the ablest
men in the body participated. Twice as many more
would gladly have engaged in the debate, but did not
secure the floor. Every speaker commended the League
in the highest terms. Each contended that his favorite
view ought to be adopted because it would surely promote the highest interests of an organization that was
worthy of the best things which the General Conference
could do for it. The chief bone of contention was
the proposition relating to affiliated societies. Another
matter concerning which there was some difference of
opinion was the creation of the office of general secretary. Several speakers thought that the duties of this
position could be performed by the Corresponding
Secretary of the Sunday School Union and Tract Society. An amendment calling for such an adjustment
was pressed. There was a more radical difference, however, on the proposition of the report to have the general secretary and the editor of *The Epworth Herald*
elected by the General Conference. This question

was debated with great zeal. It was finally resolved that the editor be elected by the General Conference and that the selection of a secretary be referred to the Board of Control. When the hour of adjournment arrived some problems concerning the financial support of the general secretary were under consideration, and the matter was referred back to the committee for adjustment.

On the Tuesday following the Epworth League again absorbed the attention of the Conference for almost the entire session. The revised report of the committee was presented. Almost immediately Dr. D. S. Monroe moved that the paragraph referring to the status of other young people's societies be stricken out. This raised a storm. It raged with increasing force for the space of an hour. But the motion finally prevailed, and the reference was expunged. Subsequently a motion to print the rejected statement as a footnote in the Discipline was carried by a unanimous vote. ●

We append the text of the General Constitution as finally adopted by the Conference. It appears as Paragraph 325 of the Discipline. Provision was also made in a carefully prepared report to harmonize other paragraphs of the Discipline with the new legislation of the Epworth League.

YOUNG PEOPLE'S SOCIETIES.

For the purpose of promoting intelligent and vital piety among the young people of our churches and congregations, and of training them in works of mercy and help, there shall be an organization under the authority of the General Conference of the Methodist Episcopal Church and governed by the following Constitution :

7

Constitution.

ARTICLE 1.   *Name.*—The title of this organization shall be "The Epworth League of the Methodist Episcopal Church."

ARTICLE 2.   *Object.*—The object of the League is to promote intelligent and vital piety in the young members and friends of the Church, to aid them in the attainment of purity of heart and constant growth in grace, and to train them in works of mercy and help.

ARTICLE 3.   *Organization.*—With a view to carry out the objects of the League, the chapters and such other young people's societies as may be approved by the Quarterly Conferences shall be organized into Presiding Elders' District Leagues, and may also be formed into General Conference District Leagues.   Other groupings may be arranged for the advantage of the work, such as Annual Conference Leagues, State Leagues, City Leagues, etc.   The chapter shall be under the control of the Quarterly Conference and pastor.   Any young people's society may become an affiliated chapter of the Epworth League, provided it adopt the aims of the League, that its president and officers and general plans of work be approved by the pastor and official board or Quarterly Conference, and that it be enrolled at the central office.*

ARTICLE 4.   *Government.*—The management of the League shall be vested in the Board of Control, to consist (1) of fifteen members appointed by the bishops, one of whom shall be a bishop, who shall be President of the Epworth League and of the Board of Control ; (2) and of one member from each General Conference district, to be chosen as the organization in each General Conference district may decide.   This Board of Control shall meet twice in each quadrennium.   When the Board of Control holds its first meeting in the quadrennium, should any General Conference district be without representation by failure to elect, the Board may elect some one from the district to represent it.

ARTICLE 5.   *Officers.*—The officers of the League shall be a president, four vice presidents—two of whom, at least, shall be laymen—a general secretary, and a treasurer, who shall constitute the General

---

* It is not hereby intended to disturb the present status of other young people's societies now organized in the Methodist Episcopal Church which are under control of the pastor and Quarterly Conference.

League Cabinet, of which the editor of *The Epworth Herald* and the German Assistant Secretary shall be members *ex officio.* The president shall be chosen as hereinbefore provided. The vice president shall be chosen by the Board of Control from their own members. The general secretary shall be elected by the Board of Control, and shall be the executive officer of the League. He shall have charge of all correspondence, and shall keep the records of the League. He shall also be editor of Epworth League publications other than *The Epworth Herald.* The treasurer shall be elected by the Board of Control. The editor of *The Epworth Herald* shall be elected by the General Conference. All these officers shall be elected quadrennially, and shall hold office until their successors are chosen. The duties of the general secretary and the editor of *The Epworth Herald* shall be performed under the direction of the Board of Control ; and the Cabinet shall act for the Board of Control *ad interim.* Vacancies in any of the above named positions, except the presidency and the editorship of the *Herald*, shall be filled by the Cabinet, subject to the approval of the Board of Control.

ARTICLE 6. *German Assistant Secretary.*—The editor of the *Haus und Herd* is constituted the German Assistant Secretary of the Epworth League, and thereby a member of the General League Cabinet.

ARTICLE 7. *Finances.*—The salaries of the editor of *The Epworth Herald* and of the general secretary shall be fixed by the Book Committee. All other expenses of the Board of Control shall be met through means which it shall devise. No collection shall be taken by the Epworth League of the Methodist Episcopal Church except for League purposes.

ARTICLE 8. *Central Office.*—The central office of the Epworth League shall be in Chicago, Ill.

ARTICLE 9. *Local Constitution.*—The Constitution for local chapters shall be in charge of the Board of Control ; *provided,* however, that no enactment shall be made which shall in any manner conflict with this General Constitution.

ARTICLE 10. *By-Laws.*—The Board of Control shall have power to enact such by-laws for its own government as will not conflict with this Constitution.

ARTICLE 11. *Amendments.*—This Constitution shall be altered or amended only by the General Conference.

We have referred to a Sabbath mass meeting. It was really a magnificent affair. In planning for a series of representative Sabbath afternoon gatherings, which made the General Conference of 1892 famous, Bishop Newman was careful that the Epworth League should be counted in. The young people of Omaha and Council Bluffs had tendered the delegates and League visitors a delightful reception on the previous evening, and this whetted the appetite of the people for the intellectual and spiritual feast they were to enjoy on Sabbath afternoon. Exposition Hall was crowded. Every foot of standing room was eagerly occupied. The officers of the First Baptist Church, near by, kindly opened their temple for an overflow meeting, and it, too, was full. Bishop Fitz-Gerald presided. Dr. J. H. Coleman prayed fervently. Chaplain McCabe—the incomparable McCabe—led the singing. Those who have heard him sing know what that means. The rapturous choruses of that afternoon seem to be ringing in our ears as we write. The speech-makers were Dr. J. L. Hurlbut, Dr. Henry Liebhart, Mr. W. H. Beach, of Jersey City; Bishop Vincent, and Bishop Warren. If each address had been prepared with special reference to all the others utterances more timely and appropriate could not have been made. The multitude was in a most responsive mood. Every taking point was enthusiastically applauded. Before the meeting closed a fraternal messenger was received from the Young Men's Christian Association of Omaha, whose cordial words were aptly responded to by Bishop War-ren. After the last hymn had been sung and the bene-diction pronounced the people still lingered. Chaplain McCabe was prevailed upon to sing again, and then Dr.

F. A. Hardin, of Chicago, exhorted a little. The power of God was signally manifested. Many were greatly blessed and went away with joy in their hearts and upon their lips. We have been assured that the meeting made a profound impression and will be the theme of conver- ᛫ sation in coming years when the experiences of the General Conference of 1892 are recounted.

The General Conference placed the responsibility of electing a general secretary upon the Board of Control. The understanding was that the Board would meet and attend to this duty without delay. But for various reasons it was found difficult to secure a meeting in the early summer. The brethren assembled on September 3, at First Church, Cleveland, O. Dr. Levi Gilbert, pastor, welcomed us in characteristic style, and the pastors and League workers of the city were unremitting in their kind attentions. Bishop FitzGerald was president, and Dr. Doherty served as secretary for the session.

A portion of the first afternoon was spent in visiting the old Central Church. It was a time of intense pleasure. Each visitor examined the historic classroom with curious interest. Then the little company was seated, and a hush fell upon all. In a moment Mr. Cooper arose and spoke most touchingly of the memorable meeting held there in May, 1889. At the close of his remarks some one started the hymn,

> " O for a thousand tongues, to sing
> My great Redeemer's praise,"

and it was sung with much feeling. Many eyes filled with tears as the triumphant notes echoed through the old building. Brother Haven then indulged in some

entertaining reminiscences, and soon led the company in
prayer.   Appropriate remarks were also made by Messrs.
Doherty, Helman, and Day, and by Rev. S. O. Royal.

On Sunday afternoon a mass meeting was held at
First Church.   It was an impromptu affair, but brimful
of life.   Dr. Levi Gilbert's inspiring new hymn, "Onward, Epworth Leaguers," was sung with spirit, and
several suggestive addresses were made.

Three sessions of the Board were held on Monday.
Much important routine business was disposed of.   A
Junior League Constitution. was adopted.   The local
Constitution was revised and some important altera-
tions made.   At the afternoon session the election of
the general officers came up.   Several brethren told
what kind of a man in their judgment the new secretary should be.   Then an informal ballot was taken.
Twenty-two ballots were cast.   Revs. W. N. Brodbeck, H. C. Jennings, C. J. North, J. H. Coleman, W.
H. W. Rees, and E. M. Mills, and Messrs. O. L. Doty,
R. R. Doherty, and H. V. Holt each received votes.
On the fifth formal ballot Dr. Brodbeck received a
majority of all the votes cast, and was declared duly
elected.   The secretary was instructed to notify the
doctor of his election, and ask his acceptance.   The
other offices of the Board were filled as follows : First
Vice President, Willis W. Cooper ; Second Vice President, Rev. W. I. Haven ; Third Vice President, R. R.
Doherty ; Fourth Vice President, Rev. H. C. Jennings ;
Treasurer, Charles E. Piper.

In the evening the Board was tendered a banquet at
the Hollenden Hotel.   It was in all respects a charm-
ing affair.   A closing business session was held on

Tuesday morning. Some of the preliminaries for the first International Conference were arranged. A League song book was authorized. The general secretary was requested to send a special letter of information and exhortation to the chapters.

The Board adjourned without having had any definite word from Dr. Brodbeck, but before most of the brethren had left the city a message came, saying that he was reluctantly compelled to decline the position. This caused disappointment and sorrow. The brethren had felt that an admirable selection had been made, and all were congratulating themselves over the great work which Dr. Brodbeck was sure to accomplish. The entire Church joined with the Board in sincere regret over the declination.

The election of a general secretary was thus thrown into the hands of the Cabinet. That body convened at the Book Concern building, New York, on November 3. A whole session was given to a patient canvass of the abilities of brethren who had been mentioned (without their consent) for the position of general secretary. Then a vote was taken, and Rev. Edwin A. Schell, pastor of First Methodist Episcopal Church, Yonkers, N. Y., was unanimously elected. Brother Schell was notified of his election, and during the afternoon accepted the position. The new secretary assumed the duties of his office immediately, and has since been tireless in his work. His first six months were spent almost wholly in the field, and everywhere large audiences listened to his eloquent addresses. His administration of the important office fully justifies the wisdom of his selection.

CHAPTER IX.

THE LEAGUE AT WORK.

THE general management of the League is vested in a Board of Control. It consists of fifteen members appointed by the bishops, one of whom shall be a bishop and President of the Epworth League and of the Board of Control ; and of one member from each General Conference district, to be chosen as the League organization in each General Conference district may decide. This Board of Control meets twice during each quadrennium. The officers of the General League are a president and four vice presidents (two of whom must be laymen), a general secretary, and a general treasurer. These officers, together with the editor of *The Epworth Herald* and the German Assistant Secretary, constitute the General League Cabinet. The president, as before stated, is chosen by the bishops. The vice presidents are elected by the Board of Control from their members. The secretary and treasurer are selected by this body also. The secretary is the executive officer of the League. The central office of the League is in Chicago.

The *personnel* of the present Board of Control is as follows : Appointed by the bishops : Bishop James N. FitzGerald, President ; Ministers—Revs. W. I. Haven, Boston, Mass.; J. H. Coleman, Troy, N. Y.; E. M. Mills, Elmira, N. Y. ; J. W. E. Bowen, Washington, D. C. ; S. O. Royal, Middletown, O. ; L. E. Prentiss, Chatta-

The Epworth League of the Methodist Episcopal Church

THIS IS TO CERTIFY

That

Connected with the

Methodist * Episcopal * Church

District, _____ Conference,

is hereby Recognized as CHAPTER No. _____ of the

Epworth League of the Methodist Episcopal Church

Organized by representatives of the Young People's Societies of the Methodist Episcopal Church, at Cleveland, Ohio, May the fifteenth, 1889, and adopted by the General Conference of the Methodist Episcopal Church, May, 1892.

For the

BOARD OF CONTROL :

J. W. Fitzgerald
President.

Edwin A. Schell
General Secretary.

FACSIMILE OF THE CHARTER OF THE EPWORTH LEAGUE OF THE METHODIST EPISCOPAL CHURCH.

nooga, Tenn.; H. C. Jennings, Red Wing, Minn.; Laymen—R. R. Doherty, New York city ; J. B. Scott, Philadelphia, Pa.; R. K. Root, Buffalo, N. Y.; H. A. Schroetter, Cincinnati, O.; N. T. De Pauw, New Albany, Ind.; C. E. Piper, Chicago; F. D. Fuller, Topeka, Kan. Elected by the General Conference District Leagues : First District, Everett O. Fisk, Boston, Mass.; Second District, C. D. Hammond, Albany, N. Y.; Third District, G. M. Colville, Binghamton, N. Y.; Fourth District, C. Roszell Cathcart, Baltimore, Md.; Fifth District, Byron E. Helman, Cleveland, O. ; Sixth District, John A. Patten, Chattanooga, Tenn.; Seventh District, Willis W. Cooper, St. Joseph, Mich.; Eighth District, W. H. W. Rees, Des Moines, Iowa; Ninth District, W. C. Jones, Black River Falls, Wis.; Tenth District, B. L. Paine, Lincoln, Neb. ; Eleventh District, Jesse B. Young, St. Louis, Mo.; Twelfth District, member to be chosen; Thirteenth District, William Koeneke, San Jose, Ill. ; Fourteenth District, —— ——. The Cabinet is at present composed as follows: President, Bishop James N. FitzGerald, New Orleans, La. ; First Vice President, W. W. Cooper, St. Joseph, Mich.; Second Vice President, William I. Haven, Boston, Mass.; Third Vice President, R. R. Doherty, New York city ; Fourth Vice President, H. C. Jennings, Red Wing, Minn.; Secretary, Edwin A. Schell, Chicago; Treasurer, C. E. Piper, Chicago ; J. F. Berry, Editor of *The Epworth Herald*, Chicago, and Henry Liebhart, Editor *Haus und Herd*, Cincinnati, O.

The forms of Epworth organization authorized by the Discipline are the General Conference District League, the Presiding Elder's District League, and the local

chapter.   The General Conference District League
has not yet been found, except in two or three notable
instances, to be of very great practical value.   The territory of the district is usually very extensive, and the
means of intercommunication are not always convenient
or adequate.   Besides, the multiplication of State and
Conference Leagues has had a tendency to diminish the
importance of the more general organization, whose
chief purpose is served in the election of a member of
the Board of Control.   The Presiding Elder's District
organization is superlatively important.   In most of the
Conferences every district has been organized, and the
work in the local chapter has thereby been systematized
and helped.   In addition to these three organizations,
which are definitely provided for in the Constitution, a
number of other forms of organization have sprung up.
It has been found advantageous in many of the larger
towns and cities to form unions in which all the chapters
of the place are enrolled.   In some cities, where the
natural divisions of the territory favor it, there are two
or more city unions, as, for instance, in Chicago, where
there is a South Side, a West Side, and a North Side
Union.   Other modifications of the city union idea may
be found, as the Tri-city Union, of which Rock Island,
Ill., Moline, Ill., and Davenport, Ia., are one instance,
and Omaha, Neb., Council Bluffs, Ia., and South Omaha,
Neb., are another.   It is now becoming customary in
rural localities to hold group meetings, or subdistrict
conventions, the theory being that a gathering of a few
neighboring chapters is of more practical value than a
larger convention.   One of the most general forms of
organization is that of the Annual Conference League.

Nearly every Conference in the connection holds a convention once a year. At the annual session of the Conference an anniversary is held. The State League has grown in favor during the last year or two. Some of the States magnify this organization to a very high degree, and receive almost unspeakable help from the conventions held under its auspices.

The working plans of the local chapter are simple enough, though the work to be accomplished is as complex as the range and ramifications of Christian activities. Members are constituted by election of the chapter, on nomination of the president, after approval by the cabinet. The pastor is *ex officio* a member of the chapter and of the cabinet. Wherever a chapter so decides, there may be two classes of members, active and associate. The active members are expected to subscribe to the following pledge :

+————————————————————————+

I will earnestly seek for myself, and do what I can to help others attain, the highest New Testament standard of experience and life. I will abstain from all those forms of worldly amusements forbidden by the Discipline of the Methodist Episcopal Church, and I will attend, so far as possible, the religious meetings of the chapter and of the Church, and take some active part in them.

+————————————————————————+

In cases where there are two classes of members the active members only are eligible to election as officers of the chapter, while associate members are entitled to all other privileges of membership. The officers are a president, four vice presidents, a secretary, and a treasurer, and these, together with the pastor and the superintendent of the Junior League, constitute the cabinet. The president must be a member of the Methodist Episcopal Church, and the other officers must be members of the Methodist Episcopal or some other evangel-

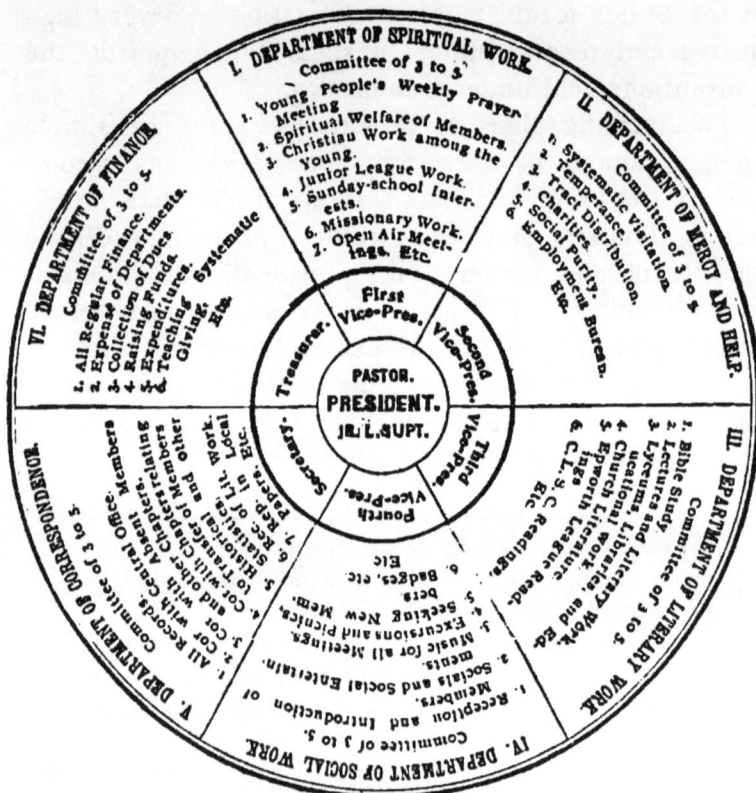

THE EPWORTH WHEEL.

ical Church. The election of the officers must be confirmed by the Quarterly Conference, of which body the president becomes a member. The Discipline makes it the duty of the president " to present to the Quarterly Conference a report of the chapter, together with such information as the Conference may require and he may be able to give."

The various phases of League work are indicated in the "Epworth Wheel," an admirable device for which Mr. B. E. Helman, of Cleveland, O., stands sponsor. It will be seen that the work of the chapter is conducted through six departments, as follows : (1) Spiritual Work ; (2) Mercy and Help ; (3) Literary Work ; (4) Social Work ; (5) Correspondence ; (6) Finance. A vice president is in charge of the work of each department, the first vice president being in charge of the Department of Spiritual Work, the second vice president of Mercy and Help, the third vice president of Literary Work, the fourth vice president of Social Work, the secretary of Correspondence, and the treasurer of Finance.

First and foremost in the sphere of Epworth work is the Department of Spiritual Work. To it is especially committed the care of the spiritual interests of the chapter. According to the provisions of the local Con-stitution it is expected to arrange for the regular prayer meetings of the chapter, and to plan special revival meet-ings and neighborhood outdoor and cottage services. It looks after the spiritual welfare of the members, inviting those who are interested to join the classes of the church. It conducts children's prayer meetings, or de-votional meetings for special classes of persons, as sail-ors, railroad men, etc. It is expected to help the super-intendent in building up the Sunday school. It also endeavors to interest the young people in the missionary enterprises of the church. To it are committed all the evangelistic and devotional activities of the chapter.

Where the work of the League is so divided that the different departments interweave their efforts, the Department of Spiritual Work always arranges for the devotional exercises in sociables, lectures, and all such meetings.

The work of the second department is, to our mind, of vital importance. Every community furnishes abundant opportunities for the Mercy and Help workers to perform their kind offices and sweet charities. A prominent feature of its work is the systematic visitation of the members of the chapter, the sick of the neighborhood, the aged and newcomers of the community. Besides, it interests the League in the charities of the place, and plans to give aid when needed. It has charge of temperance work, social purity work, and tract distribution. All kinds of charitable duties, when undertaken by the chapter, such as visiting hospitals, nursing, distributing flowers, starting industrial schools, running employment bureaus, coffee houses, day nurseries, etc., are under its care.

The Department of Literary Work aims to encourage the young people in the study of the Scriptures, and to instruct them in the doctrines, polity, history, and present activities of the Methodist Episcopal Church, and of the other denominations of the Church universal, and to give stimulus and direction to general Christian culture. It has charge of all courses of reading and study pursued by the chapter. It may open, whenever practicable, libraries, reading rooms, art rooms, and night schools. It arranges for lectures and literary gatherings, at which members of the chapter and others present essays, papers, talks, debates, etc. It endeavors to extend the circulation of the books and papers of the Church, and to do what it can to quicken the intellectual life of its members and the community.

To the Department of Social Work is assigned the important and delightful duty of seeking and receiving new members. It is commissioned to introduce such features as will develop the highest and best social life. It has charge of the social parts of all gatherings. The music of the chapter and its entertainments, other than the literary programs, are under its care. These young workers provide flowers for the pulpit, ushers when needed, and attend to procuring badges, emblems, banners, decorations, etc., and are the custodians of all such effects belonging to the chapter. Picnics, excursions, and the like are naturally under the care of the Department of Social Work.

The Secretary and his assistants are expected to keep a record of the membership, of the meetings, and of all courses of reading and study pursued. It is desirable that they send reports of the meetings of the chapter to local papers. Also that they keep copies of all programs, newspapers, and other notices of the chapter's affairs, and all memorabilia relating to its doings. This department may carry on correspondence with the central and district offices, and is the custodian of all records. By it members in good standing are recommended to other Leagues.

The last of the departments performs such duties as usually devolve upon the treasurer. It is supposed to present to the chapter plans for meeting its financial needs. It collects all dues and receives all moneys, disbursing the same as the chapter may direct. All

matters involving an expenditure of money are referred
to this department for consideration before the final
action of the chapter.

Work in at least one of these divisions is assigned to
every member. He may choose his special field of
activity, but having chosen it he is expected to be loyal
to his department superintendent and render in all
cases the best possible service.

THE JUNIOR EPWORTH LEAGUE.

One of the most interesting and vital features of
League work is that which pertains to the care and culture of the children. For this special purpose the
Junior Epworth League was established. Its scheme
of work is a modification and adaptation of that
of the Epworth League. Its chief officer is the superintendent, who is appointed by the pastor, and who is
also a member of the Epworth League cabinet. The
other officers are a president, four vice presidents, a
treasurer, and a secretary, who are elected by the Juniors
from among their own number, and these, with the superintendent and pastor, constitute the Junior League
cabinet. The membership is made up of boys and
girls under fourteen years of age.

The "Junior Wheel" is the suggestion of Rev. N. J.
Harkness, of the Rock River Conference, a most successful worker among the little men and women. Like
the Senior one, it is divided into six sections. Each of
these divisions has a key-word indicating something of
its purpose.

The key-word of the first department is *heart*. It
stands for the development of true heart life. The con-

version of the children is the chief aim of every Junior superintendent. After there is evidence that the child has accepted the Saviour there should follow plain teaching in Christian doctrine and instruction in practical

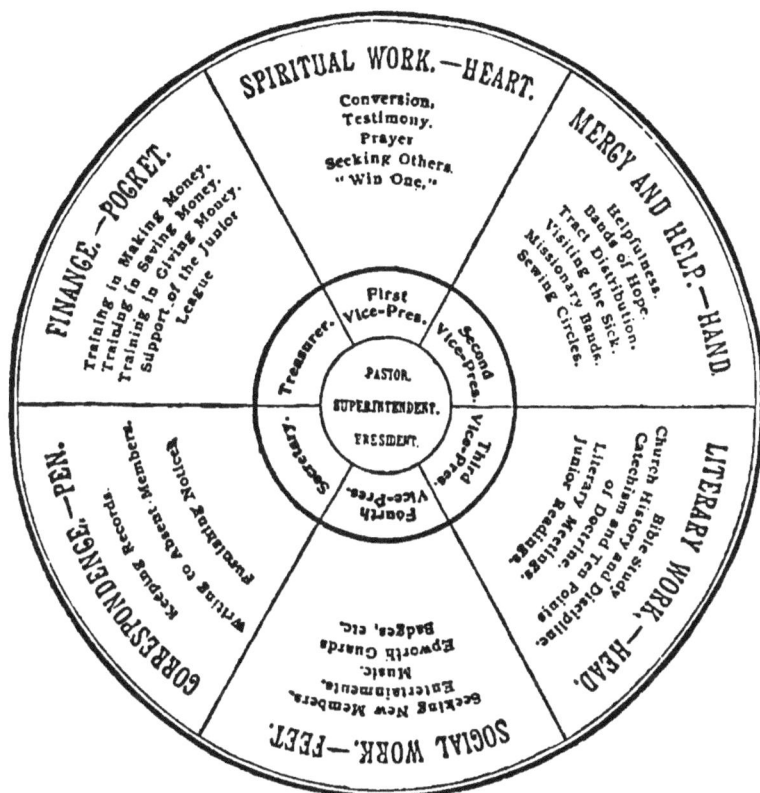

SPIRITUAL WORK.—HEART.
Conversion.
Testimony.
Prayer
Seeking Others.
"Win One."

MERCY AND HELP.—HAND.
Helpfulness.
Bands of Hope.
Tract Distribution.
Visiting the Sick.
Missionary Bands.
Sewing Circles.

FINANCE.—POCKET.
Training in Making Money.
Training in Saving Money.
Training in Giving Money.
Support of the Junior League.

First Vice-Pres.
Treasurer.
Second Vice-Pres.
PASTOR.
SUPERINTENDENT.
PRESIDENT.
Third Vice-Pres.
Fourth Vice-Pres.
Secretary.

LITERARY WORK.—HEAD.
Church History and Discipline.
Bible Study.
Catechism and Ten Points.
Literary Meetings.
Junior Readings.

CORRESPONDENCE.—PEN.
Keeping Records.
Writing to Absent Members.
Sending Notices.

SOCIAL WORK.—FEET.
Badges, etc.
Epworth Guards.
Music.
Entertainments.
Seeking New Members.

THE JUNIOR WHEEL.

religious duties. The children are urged to take part in their own devotional meetings. They are encouraged to testify and lead in short, simple prayers. Besides, they are shown how to bring their young friends to the Master.
8

The key-word of Department Two is *hand.* The idea which it represents is that of helpfulness. Various kinds of Mercy and Help work are undertaken under the guidance of the intelligent superintendent, and the children are made very happy by the knowledge that they are putting light and joy into lives that have been full of darkness and sorrow.

Department Three has for its key-word *head.* This suggests thoughtfulness and study. Great interest is taken by the little people in the systematic study of the Bible as a book. Many of them can readily give the names of the different books, and the order in which they appear, as well as the name of the author and the circumstances under which the book was written. There are also drills in the history of our own Church, in the "ten points of doctrine" and Catechism. Literary meetings are held occasionally with great profit, the aim being to secure correct habits of thought and a taste for good literature.

Department Four is assigned to social work. The key-word is *feet.* The children are encouraged to seek out those of their companions who are not identified with the League or some similar society, and bring them in. In many ways they provide innocent and delightful recreation for each other and for their grown-up friends. The fifth and sixth departments embrace the usual duties of secretary and treasurer.

The first Junior League registered at the central office was that of First Church, Hoboken, N. J., Rev. C. R. Barnes, D.D., pastor; the second was that of Keyser, W. Va., and the third that of Asbury Church, Des Moines, Ia. Other Leagues were formed almost immediately, and they soon began to spring up all over the land. The four years of Junior development and success have been scarcely less marvelous than the record made by the Seniors. It is now a splendid army marching many thousand strong. It has no lack of ardent friends. Many of our most successful church workers properly praise its practical achievements. New plans are constantly being devised for the entertainment, instruction, and spiritual culture of the little people. *The Junior Herald* is a two-page weekly supplement to *The Epworth Herald*, and is given up exclusively to the promotion of their work. At least two columns of reports from Junior Leagues are printed each week. These are written by the Juniors themselves, and show a remarkable comprehension of the design and plans of their organization.

CHAPTER X.

EPWORTH LEAGUE EXTENSION.

THE Epworth League is branching out. Months ago it swept beyond the boundaries of the Methodist Episcopal Church and found a warm welcome in at least three other branches of the great Methodist family. And why not? Was the organization not needed in these sister churches as much as it was in our own? Is it not as well adapted to promote the social, intellectual, and spiritual culture of their young people as it is those within our own fold? Yea, verily. As the aims and methods of our young organization become more generally known it will still grow in favor, and will eventually become as world-wide as Methodism itself.

THE LEAGUE IN THE METHODIST EPISCOPAL CHURCH, SOUTH.

At the General Conference held at St. Louis, Mo., it was decided to form " young people's leagues having for their object the promotion of piety and loyalty to our Church, education in church history, and their encouragement in works of grace and charity." The responsible work of preparing the way for such a society was intrusted to the General Sunday School Committee. This committee was composed of W. G. E. Cunnyngham, chairman; T. J. Magruder, J. H. Carlisle, G. A. Dazey, J. D. Hamilton, and J. R. Pepper. These de-

voted brethren met at Nashville, Tenn., December 18,
1890, and, after long and prayerful deliberation, adopted
the Epworth League as the official young people's society of the Methodist Episcopal Church, South. The
name " Epworth League " was selected, the brethren
declared, for these reasons : " (1) Because of its historical associations. It carried the mind back to the birthplace and early home of the founder of Methodism.
The name also recalls the family life and godly training
of the Wesley home, an example worthy to be kept in
perpetual remembrance. (2) Because of its ecumenical
character, being common to all the many branches of
Wesleyan Methodism in this country, in Europe, and in
all countries where it exists. From Epworth as a geo-
graphical center its lines have gone out through all the
earth, and its words unto the end of the world." The
form of the organization is a modification of that of the
League of the Methodist Episcopal Church. The membership consists of "all persons over fifteen years, of
good moral character, who are willing to obey the rules
and regulations of the League and do any work assigned
them." All officers must be members of the Methodist
Episcopal Church, South. The work is divided into
three departments instead of six, namely, Christian Effort, Charity and Help, and Literary Work. Up to the
present time about eight hundred local chapters have
been reported to the central office at Nashville. Many
chapters are known to be in existence that have not been
formally enrolled, so that it is safe to say that there are
now upward of a thousand all told. The churches in
the cities and larger towns have been quite generally
organized, and in some cases those in rural regions have

also taken up the work with a due measure of zeal. Special stress has everywhere been placed upon the Department of "Charity and Help," and a work has been done the recital of which would thrill any heart with joy. That the work has not moved more rapidly than it has may be accounted for by the fact that much of the constituency of the Methodist Episcopal Church, South, is rural. A rural population is always slowly converted to new ideas and new institutions.

The Texas Leagues were first to form a State organization. The good example has been followed by California, Missouri, and Alabama. The Leagues of Tennessee met recently and planned for the enthusiastic extension of the work. There is now much talk of a council of all the Leagues in Southern Methodism at an early day. It has been our good fortune to meet some of the most influential leaders in our sister Church, and we have been delighted with their expressions of cordial approval of the Epworth League. It is, they declare, supplying a "long-felt want," and supplying it well. The denomination is just beginning to realize something of the bigness and value of the movement. Rapid and substantial advance is now certain. The work has been under the superintendence of Dr. W. G. E. Cunnyngham, the efficient Sunday school secretary. It could not have fallen into better hands. The doctor is an Epworth enthusiast. He believes in the League with all his heart. He regards it as a movement destined to do marvelous things for the young Methodists of the South, and is throwing great energy into the work of directing and inspiring the young leaders. The *Epworth Methodist,* an independent paper, has been pub-

lished at Fort Worth, Texas, for some time, and the
little organ is rendering valuable service to the cause.
In due time a regular official organ will, no doubt, be
commissioned.   In the meantime the various *Advocates*
are devoting generous space to the growing cause, and
the editors are vying with each other in paying to this
grand army of young people tributes of appreciation
and praise.

THE LEAGUE IN CANADA.

For years the need of some comprehensive young
people's organization was felt in Canadian Methodism.
Of course there were the usual literary and social societies, but these had no cohesion or unity, and had not
much direct religious influence.   At the General Conference of 1882 Rev. W. H. Withrow, D.D., introduced
a resolution calling for the organization of a young
people's society with definite reading courses, somewhat
after the plan of the Church Lyceum of the Methodist
Episcopal Church.   This was received with a good deal
of favor, a course of reading was arranged, and a number of reading unions were organized.   The plan, however, did not take like fire among the heather.   When
Dr. Withrow returned from Europe in September, 1889,
he learned from our press of the organization of the
Epworth League.   " Here," he said, " is the very thing
needed for Canadian Methodism."   He sent at once
for our leaflets and mailed them to Rev. Dr. Carman,
general superintendent, and other men of light and
leading in the Church.   He also brought the new movement to the attention of the Sunday School Board, which
met in October, but the brethren did not seem to appre-
hend the importance of the matter.   One or two said

they had received the leaflets, but threw them into the
waste-paper basket. Another suggested that the matter
be postponed for a year, till the meeting of the General
Conference in 1890. But the doctor said, " If the thing
is good why waste a year ? why not adopt it now ?" The
general superintendent, who heartily sympathized with
the movement, called a representative committee to
consider the matter forthwith, the Constitution of our
American League was adopted with slight modifications
to suit Canadian needs, and a copious supply of literature was ordered printed. The movement was formally
inaugurated in a mass meeting held in the Metropolitan
Church, Toronto. That large building was filled to the
doors. Vigorous addresses were given, and the plan
adopted with enthusiasm. The leading papers ably
seconded the movement with editorial comments and
commendations. Subsequent mass meetings were held
in Hamilton, London, and elsewhere. The new departure was hailed with delight by many ministers and
young laymen, who cordially cooperated in these opening meetings. The subsequent history of the movement
has been one of notable progress. It should be mentioned that before Dr. Withrow's return in the summer
of 1889 one chapter was formed auxiliary to the League
in this country—that in Barrie, Ontario. It was organized by the Rev. R. N. Burns, B.A., a successful
youngerly minister, who also held the first League convention, in that town.

A few of the ministers who held official relations to
the Young People's Society of Christian Endeavor ob-
jected to the new League as a divisive force, but their
objections carried little weight. At the General Confer-

ence of 1890 the League was recognized as an integral department of the Methodist Church of Canada, and provision was made that its presidents be, by virtue of office, members of the Quarterly Board. This is the first recognition in the world, we believe, of the League as an organic part of the Church. At that Conference it was proposed that direct affiliation should take place with the Christian Endeavor Society, and the name of "Epworth League of Christian Endeavor" was suggested as an official name. That proposition the General Conference did not sanction. A Constitution, however, was adopted embodying a pledge and principles in harmony with those of the Endeavor Society, which it was thought would facilitate friendly affiliation with that body. But as the Endeavor Society insisted on the adoption of the name as well, a committee of the General Conference made it possible for individual societies, if they chose, to adopt the name "Epworth League of Christian Endeavor," in the hope of uniting all the young people's societies under one comprehensive organization. That expectation, however, has not been realized. Writing to us recently, Dr. Withrow says :

A very large number of Epworth Leagues have become Epworth Leagues of Christian Endeavor, but a very small number of Endeavor societies in our Church have reciprocated by affiliation on the same basis. My opinion is that the double relationship is cumbersome and burdensome, the affiliated Leagues being expected to contribute to the finances of both organizations and to help in sustaining the provincial and international conventions and local unions of the two bodies.

In company with Mr. Willis W. Cooper it was our privilege to attend the General Conference held at Mon-

treal mentioned above. We were received with marked
courtesy by the members of the committee having Epworth League interests in charge. They were eager to
learn of the practical workings of the League in the
United States, and we gave such facts and suggestions
as we could. On the day following our arrival this
writer was introduced to the Conference and made a
brief address outlining the aims and methods of the Epworth League, and giving some of the benefits already
apparent in this country.

The growth of our glorious cause in Canada has been
more than satisfactory. It has extended to every prov-
ince, even to far-away Bermuda. At the present writing
there are upward of one thousand Epworth Leagues and
Epworth Leagues of Christian Endeavor. *Onward*,
the sprightly and popular newspaper organ, was started
two years ago, and already has a circulation of between
35,000 and 40,000. Two great conventions have been
held, one in March of 1892 and the other in the same
month of 1893. We accepted an invitation to be present at the first gathering, held jointly at the Metropolitan and Queen Street churches in Toronto. It was a
large and helpful convention. Crowds gathered at all
the sessions. We have never stood before more recep-
tive and inspiring congregations. Dr. Withrow is editor
of *Onward*, and in connection with his duties as Sunday school secretary is also major general of the League.
A Methodist Young People's Association, embracing
all young people's societies in the Church, has been
formed, and is accomplishing a good work. Mr. R. W.
Dillion, of Toronto, is the energetic secretary, and Mr.
F. W. Daly, of London, the president.

THE LEAGUE IN MANY LANDS.

Several chapters have been organized in the Wesleyan churches of England, and are doing satisfactory work. Our friends yonder assure us that the movement will necessarily be of slow growth, but that the methods of the League are as well adapted to the churches there as here. The general adoption of our organization, or some modification of it, is only a question of a little time. In our European missions the cause is growing rapidly. In Norway and Sweden we have many flourishing chapters. In Italy our cause has taken firm hold. The struggling Bulgarian Mission is pushing the work. In the India Conferences encouraging advance has been made. Bishop Mallalieu says the League is a positive spiritual force in the churches there. In China we have several chapters, and in Japan a good start has recently been made. The work in Mexico, and in our South American missions has opened auspiciously. The Methodist Episcopal Church, South, has also introduced the League into its missions in Japan and elsewhere, and they are cooperating with us in a forward movement, which will soon establish our cause firmly in every land where we have gone in the name of the Lord to plant the Methodist standard. A backward look fills one with wonder and gratitude. A look into the future makes one joyful because of the certainty of more glorious conquests.

CHAPTER XI.

SOME HAPPY RESULTS.

THE Epworth League has already shown practical results which abundantly justify its existence. To hundreds of communities it has brought precious benedictions. Pastors wonder how they managed to get along without it so long. The young people are *at work*. Many of them are being singularly blessed in their undertakings. It will be interesting to note in this closing chapter a few of the more striking results of the four years of League endeavor.

No careful observer will question the fact that the League has promoted denominational loyalty. The *name* of our society has stimulated widespread inquiry into Methodist traditions and history. Our young people have learned about Epworth and the famous family which lived there, as well as the stirring events connected with the beginnings of Methodism. They have become more familiar, too, with the doctrines which John Wesley preached and Charles Wesley sang. Naturally enough, they have inquired concerning the polity of the great Church, the history of which in England and America has so greatly interested them. Indeed, our young people all over the world are studying the *why* of Methodism with a zeal never before known. This will attach them more closely to the Church of their fathers and render less successful the efforts of that docile and lamblike individual who, with great amiability of manner and softness of speech, is ever going about upon the outskirts of our fold "seeking whom he may devour." We refer to the systematic proselyter. By this it is not meant that our young people are becoming bigoted. That is a state of mind which our host abhors. We love other churches none the less because we are ardently attached to our own.

Through its Department of Mercy and Help the League has emphasized the practical side of the Christian life. Good Samaritan duties have been made prominent. We have tried to show that true religion makes us self-forgetting and sends us out to minister to the needy and suffering. We have laid to heart the apostle's command, "Bear ye one another's burdens," and have sought opportunities to put sunshine into dark lives and to lift up the fallen. Thus have we been brought into harmony with "the law of Christ," and have known much of the joy of "going about doing good." Many people have received the impression that the Church is unsympathetic and cold—that it is intended for those who rank well in society and business. This is an error. The Church is not unsympathetic. She desires to reach the masses and do them good. The difficulty is that we have often had a poor way of showing it. But we are doing better. Brigades of sunny-faced, warm-hearted young people have determined that their Church shall be misunderstood no longer. They are going out into highways and lanes with words of mercy and deeds of helpfulness, and are compelling the multitude to crowd to the gospel feast.

Then the League has helped to solve for many

churches the problem of social amusements. It is a delicate question—none more so. What pastor has not at some time been embarrassed by it? What church has not wondered what to do? There are reasons why the Methodist Episcopal Church has often had more unrest over the amusement question than some others. Our Discipline talks plainly upon the subject. It is specific. In reference to dancing, card-playing, and the like it says, " Thou shalt not." Now, the League indorses every prohibition of the Discipline, and has never sought to apologize for the attitude of the Church. But at the same time it recognizes the fact that the young people need recreation. To meet this reasonable demand it has furnished diversion in the shape of useful occupation, and through its Department of Social Work has suggested numerous forms of social enjoyment that are free from evil influences. In this way many young people have been won from associations and practices that were leading them to ruin.

The League has also called attention to the sensational and worthless literature in circulation, and has emphasized the danger of acquiring a taste for it. It has taken out of the hands of many boys and girls dissipating books and put in their places those of a pure, solid, upbuilding character. Hundreds of reading circles have been formed. League libraries have been established. Reading rooms have been opened. A regular reading course has been provided. Entertaining lectures have been arranged. The systematic study of the English Bible has been popularized. The habit of reading devotional literature has been revived. Hundreds of young people are experiencing an uplift in their mental life of which they had not previously even dreamed. Our college presidents say that hosts of young people have begun a college course because of the stimulus given them by the Epworth movement. Because of increasing intelligence concerning the great benevolences of the Church an era of systematic giving has already dawned which will bless the Church unspeakably for generations to come. To-morrow the heart of every bishop and secretary and pastor will be thrilled by the sight of overflowing church treasuries.

Finally, the League has already proved a most effective evangelistic force. We have sought to place our spiritual work at the very front. The doctrines of "repentance" and "the witness of the Spirit" have been everywhere emphasized. We have tried to show the young people that conversion is a wonderful experience—that it means more than holding up a hand or signing a card in a revival service. "Holiness to the Lord" has been written upon our bright new banners. The privilege of the believer to be saved even to the utmost, and to be made perfect in love in this life, has become a cardinal point in our everyday creed. This organization was born in a classroom, amid prayers and tears and shouts. That was a good beginning, and much of the spirit of that hour lingers with us still. Our pastors gladly testify to the usefulness of their consecrated young people as soul-winners. In many of the revival services the young people have taken charge of the singing. In some places they have arrested attention by holding street services, and then have invited the curious crowd to accompany them to the church. In other places they have conducted a systematic house-

to-house visitation, and by their earnest appeals have
aroused the community from religious indifference. In
many cases our members have labored at the altar
with seekers or conducted inquiry meetings, and with
marked faithfulness stood by the pastor throughout the
long revival campaign. The Church has watched the
record with solicitude and joy. O, it has been *wonderful, wonderful!*

But do not dangers threaten us? No doubt. We
have been impressed with some of them while writing
these pages. Chief among them is the tendency to rely
upon mere organization. Approved machinery is good.
He who makes use of inferior appliances when better
ones are at hand is not wise. There is widespread
satisfaction with Epworth plans. The test of four years
has demonstrated their fitness. But we need more
than good machinery. We might place on the track the
mightiest locomotive ever built; we might attach it to
the longest train to which a locomotive was ever hitched;
we might burnish every brazen mounting until it
glistened with brightness; we might smooth every
journal box and oil every bearing—we could do all
this with the mightiest engine ever built, and yet it
would be a great lifeless, useless thing. But let the fires
once be kindled under the boiler, let the steam go
coursing through its iron arteries—then you have a
thing of life, a marvel of mighty power. The Epworth
"wheel" is as perfect a piece of machinery as one
could desire. But there is no power in the "wheel."
We need more. The fire must fall from above. The
energy of the divine Spirit must come to us. We
must be permeated and filled with the Pentecostal

baptism. Then shall we have power. Possessing it we shall move forward harmoniously, victoriously, in our great work. Our burdens will be light. Our most difficult duties will be easy. Our toil will be no longer toil, but a gladsome privilege—a joyous play of the soul.

9

THE END.

www.ingramcontent.com/pod-product-compliance
Lightning Source LLC
Chambersburg PA
CBHW030601270326
41927CB00007B/1002